The Triune God
An Ecumenical Study

by

E. L. Mascall

PRINCETON THEOLOGICAL MONOGRAPH SERIES

Dikran Y. Hadidian

General Editor

10

THE TRIUNE GOD

An Ecumenical Study

The Triune God
An Ecumenical Study
by
E. L. Mascall D.D., F.B.A
Professor Emeritus of Historical Theology, King's College, London

> O Trinity uncreated and without beginning,
> O undivided Unity, three and one,
> Father, Son and Spirit, a single God;
> Accept this our hymn from tongues of clay
> As if from mouths of flame.
>
> *Lenten Triodion of the Orthodox Church*

PICKWICK PUBLICATIONS
An imprint of *Wipf and Stock Publishers*
199 West 8th Avenue • Eugene OR 97401

TO MY BRETHREN OF
THE ORATORY OF THE GOOD SHEPHERD

FROM WHOM THROUGH NEARLY HALF A CENTURY
I HAVE RECEIVED
MORE THAN I CAN EVER REPAY

Pickwick Publications
An imprint of Wipf and Stock Publishers
199 West 8th Avenue, Suite 3
Eugene, Oregon 97401

The Triune God
An Ecumenical Study by E.L. Mascall
By Mascall, E. L.
Copyright©1986 by Mascall, E.L.
ISBN: 0-915138-96-4
Publication date 1/1/1986

CONTENTS

	Foreword	7
I	Relations in the Trinity: Augustine and the West	11
II	Depersonalising the Deity – The Reaction of the East	24
III	The Anonymous Spirit	34
IV	The Trinity and the World	44
V	'– and from the Son': New Thought on an Old Dispute	57
VI	Light from the Logicians	74

FOREWORD

'In speaking almost casually of "the grace of the Lord Jesus Christ and the love of God and the communion of the Holy Ghost" he [that is, St Paul] simply sums up the working faith of the Christian community.' Those words were written by Dr E. J. Bicknell in 1919 in a work which became the doctrinal pabulum of generations of the Anglican clergy[1]; they were repeated unchanged in the revision of that work by Dr H. J. Carpenter in 1955.[2] They are, I believe, profoundly true; and, in spite of the attempts of some recent academic theologians to maintain that the primitive church was, or at any rate ought to have been, unitarian in its belief, I would hold that there is a line of homogeneous development from the implicit but definite trinitarianism of the text from St Paul just quoted to the explicit and systematic teaching of documents such as the so-called Athanasian Creed. I shall not repeat the story of that devolopment; it has been recounted by many scholars more learned and competent than I. What I want to stress is that the discussion is still a living one. While I believe that the basic confessions of the faith are to be accepted with humility and gratitude – they were the work of the

[1] *A Theological Introduction to the Thirty-nine Articles of the Church of England* (Longmans), 46.
[2] 3rd ed., 35.

Spirit striving with human minds in Christ's body the Church and were sealed with blood of the martyrs – their dynamic fruitfulness is, in my experience, a perpetual source of new and exciting discoveries. So far from being quaint relics of purely antiquarian interest, they have unexpected implications in previously unexplored areas of human concern, they come to new life in bypaths where to all appearance they seemed to have reached a dead end, and from time to time they link on in an invigorating way to new advances in the secular sciences and in philosophy.

This is the explanation of the somewhat untidy shape of this book. What it quite definitely is *not* is a systematic treatise on the doctrine of the Trinity; if it were that it would have to begin further back than with St Augustine. It is the outcome of several things that have come together in my mind. The most important is the discovery that what had been for centuries the most obstinate doctrinal barrier between the Eastern and Western Churches and had been in what might be described, by a mixture of metaphors, as a chronic condition of entrenched ankylosis – the notorious '*Filioque* Controversy' – had suddenly become mobile, and this not through a mood of despairing surrender or exhausted indifference on the part of either or both of the parties but by a remarkable deepening of understanding. Then, again, I had a growing conviction that St Augustine's development of Aristotle's category of *relation*, which he had used to great effect in his discussion of the Holy Trinity and which Fr Jean Galot had quite recently extended into the field of Christology[1] might contain still unexploited riches. In particular the view, which I had already applied to several theological topics, that *relations*, if properly understood, could be just as metaphysically real and concrete as *attributes*,[2] seemed to me to be capable of further, and fully orthodox, exploration.

Furthermore, in an earlier book I had hinted at 'the possible theological utility of the advances in the logic of relations initiated by Bertrand Russell and A. N. Whitehead, especially with regard to polyadic relations', and I made the somewhat enigmatic and oracular suggestion that, 'if handled with the subtlety with which St Augustine handled Aristotle's *Categories*, this might be helpful for triadology and especially the *Filioque* dispute – or, of course, it might not.'[3] I slightly elaborated the point in an obscurely located and compressed point in a later work,[4] but, as far as I know the invitation has never been accepted. This is not surprising, but the more recent appearance of the symposium *Spirit of God, Spirit of Christ*, with the subtitle 'Ecumenical Reflections on the *Filioque* Controversy', which is both serious and constructive, treating the matter at issue neither as trivial on the one hand nor as providing useful ammunition on the other, has stimulated me to take up my own challenge. This is what I have attempted in the final chapter of this book, and I think Bertrand Russell would be surprised

[1] See my discussion in *Theology and the Gospel of Christ* (SPCK 1977), 151ff.
[2] ibid., ch. iv.
[3] ibid., 230f.
[4] *Whatever Happened to the Human Mind?* (SPCK 1980), 165 n. 9.

to find that he had, however unintentionally made a contribution to Christian theology. If some readers are dismayed by the occurrence of symbolic formulas, they may be reassured that these are there simply for economy of expression and clarity of thought; no knowledge of mathematics is required! And I think those who are willing to make the slight mental effort that is needed will be as delighted as I was to discover this fresh example of the sound Christian principle that grace does not repudiate nature but uses and transforms it.

There is a story of a well brought-up Christian who had undertaken to instruct an enquiring friend in the mystery of the Holy Trinity. 'It's really quite simple', he explained, 'You see, Three is One and One is Three.' 'I'm afraid,' the other objected, 'that I don't quite understand.' 'Ah,' his instructor triumphantly replied, 'That's the mystery.'

Perhaps all that was really wrong with that answer is that it was made at the beginning of the conversation and not at the end.

E.L.M

I

Relations in the Trinity: Augustine and the West

The starting point must be St Augustine's adoption and transformation, in developing his doctrine of the triune God,[1] of Aristotle's category of 'relation'. For Aristotle, *relation* is one of the ten 'categories' or, as the scholastics called them, 'predicaments', that is, the ten modes in which a term may be predicated of a subject. These are listed as substance, quantity, quality, relation, place, time, position, state, action and passion; and, without arguing the adequacy of this classification or settling the precise meaning of each item, it must be noted that substance has a status different from, and prior to, all the other categories. It cannot be predicated of any other category, but other categories are predicated of it. Passing from the logical to the real order, this means that substances are not inherent in attributes but attributes are inherent in them. In other words, all the other nine categories are 'accidental'; only substance is 'substantial'. To give an example, in Aristotle's sense the Albert Memorial is a 'substance', but its size and shape, its location, its distance from the Albert Hall, its date of erection, its aesthetic character and its cost all 'might have been different'; in their various ways they are all 'accidents'. Now, asked Augustine, in what category are we to place the three Persons of the Godhead, the Father,

[1] *De Trinitate*, V, v.

the Son and the Holy Spirit? We cannot say that they are three substances (three *ousiai* in Greek), for that would be tritheism; there are, it has been agreed, three persons in *one substance* (three *hypostases* in one *ousia*). But we are cannot say that they accidents, for that would imply the Sabellian heresy, that the persons are only mutable and impermanent phenomena. What was Augustine to do? He observed that one of the accidental categories, namely relation, has a very different status from the others; while, like them, it is predicated of a subject, unlike them it involves another term as well. To say that John is ugly involves nobody but John, but to say that John is uglier than Paul, while it is a statement about John and not about Paul, brings Paul into the picture as well; and it involves another relational statement, namely that Paul is less ugly than John. Now Augustine's stroke of genius was to locate the three Persons in the category of relation, while at the same time raising them from the level of accidents to the level of substance; he thus introduced the notion of person as *subsistent relation* or, as Fr Jean Galot has preferred to say in his brilliant use of it in the realm of Christology, *relational being*.[1]

The immediate reaction of many to this device of Augustine's will be to dismiss it as nothing but a clever dialectical dodge. It will also be felt that to demote the three divine Persons to the level of relations is really to depersonalize them, and it will seem to be merely a frivolous repartee if the reply is made that we do

[1] *La Personne du Christ* (Gembloux, Duculot 1969), passim. Cf my discussion in *Theology and the Gospel of Christ*, 151f.

commonly refer in ordinary speech to certain persons as our 'relations'. And in fact the accusation of depersonalizing the Godhead is often brought against Latin theologians, and Augustine is usually blamed for it. That erudite Russian lay theologian Vladimir Lossky, who combined a sweetly charitable disposition with a rocklike adherence to the tradition of Orthodoxy, wrote:

> In expounding the dogma of the Trinity, western thought most frequently took as its starting point the one nature, and thence passed to the consideration of the three persons, while the Greeks followed the opposite course – from the three persons to the one nature.... Human thought does not run the risk of going astray if it passes from the consideration of the three persons to that of the common nature.[1]

And he quoted the great authority Fr de Régnon to this effect:

> Latin philosophy first considers the nature in itself and proceeds to the agent; Greek philosophy first considers the agent and afterwards passes through it to find the nature. The Latins think of personality as a mode of nature; the Greeks think of nature as the content of the person.[2]

And, much later, the distinguished Jesuit Fr Karl Rahner, in a highly idiosyncratic exposition of trinitarian doctrine, starting from the principle of 'the free gratuitous self-communication of God to the spiritual creature in Jesus Christ and in the "Spirit"', has written:

---

[1] *The Mystical Theology of the Eastern Church* (James Clarke 1957), 56.
[2] *Etudes de Théologie positive sur la Ste Trinité*, I, 433, cit. Lossky, 57f.

> We say 'of God', and we do not presuppose thereby a 'Latin' theology of the Trinity (as contrasted with the Greek one), but the Biblical theology of the Trinity (hence, in a sense, the Greek one.)[1]

Rahner's general background and outlook is certainly 'western' and it is therefore noteworthy that his discussion has been warmly commended by the very sensitive Orthodox theologian Dr John Meyendorff.[2] After which, it is refreshing to return to Lossky and find him writing, immediately after the passage already quoted:

> Nevertheless, the two ways were both equally legitimate so long as the first did not attribute to the essence a supremacy over the three persons, nor the second to the three persons a supremacy over the common nature.... The nature is inconceivable apart from the persons or as anterior to the three persons, even in the logical order. If the balance of this antinomy between nature and persons, absolutely different and absolutely identical at the same time, is upset, there will be in the one case a tendency towards a Sabellian unitarianism (the God-essence of the philosophers), or else towards tritheism.[3]

Lossky goes on to remark that 'the Greeks saw in the formula of the procession of the Holy Spirit from the Father and the Son a tendency to stress the unity of nature at the expense of the real distinction between the persons.' This diagnosis was characteristic of Lossky, who had an attractive tendency to trace almost everything that was wrong in the West to the *Filioque*.

---

[1] *The Trinity* (Burns & Oates 1970), 83.

[2] *Christ in Eastern Christian Thought* (Washington, D.C., Corpus Books, 1969), 165f.

[3] *Mystical Theology* ..., 56f.

We shall have to consider it later.[1] At the moment we must get back to Augustine and subsistent relations.

When, in the doctrinal upheavals of the fourth century, the Church's faith was clarified and reaffirmed in the creeds of the great councils of Nicaea and Constantinople, in 325 and 381 respectively,[2] the basic principles of the Church's trinitarian belief became explicit. They were two. First was the literal and unqualified deity of each of the three Persons; the Son was of the same order of being (*homoousios*) as the Father, the Spirit was the Lord and life-giver co-worshipped and conglorified with the Father and the Son. As the *Quicunque vult* would say, with stark and paradoxical simplicity, 'the Father is God, the Son God, the Holy Spirit God; and yet not three gods but there is one God'. But the second principle is that there is an order among the three, in spite of their equality; indeed, we might say that their equality is a consequence of their order. It is *because* the Son is begotten by the Father that he is equal to the Father; it is *because* the Spirit proceeds from the Father that he is God no less than the Father is God. And it must be noticed that, while the Creed, on the pattern of the baptismal formula from which it is almost certainly elaborated, is divided into three sections corresponding to the three Persons, it begins by professing belief in One God, whom it does not describe as the Trinity but

[1] Cf pp. 57ff infra.
[2] I leave aside the question whether the so-called 'Nicene' or 'Niceno-Constantinopolitan' creed was actually promulgated at Constantinople in 381. The Council of Chalcedon in 451 certainly thought it was. Cf J. N. D. Kelly, *Early Christian Creeds* (Longmans 1950), ch. x.

as the Father, and only then goes on to declare that the Father has eternally begotten the Son and has breathed forth the Spirit. We are in fact faced with the notion of *derived equality*, and it is not an easy one to accept, as the history of the Arian and Macedonian heresies shows. The distinction between begottenness and createdness was difficult to draw, and not least because in Greek the words for uncreated and unbegotten, *agenetos* and *agennetos* respectively, differed only by a single letter. In a now forgotten book, published in 1956,[1] I argued that, on the cardinal points of Christian belief, orthodoxy consists in holding together two notions which might well seem to be mutually incompatible, but that if we enquire how they must be understood if they are *not* to be incompatible, we shall acquire a much more profound understanding of the question at issue than we had when we began. And I instanced the notion of derived equality in connection with the doctrine of the Trinity as an example of this. But behind this problem of equality, though closely connected with it, is the problem of sheer multiplicity. Whatever *Quicunque vult*[2] may say, if each of the Persons is God, how can there not be three Gods? This was the problem to which the Cappadocian Fathers, St Basil the Great and the two St Gregories, addressed themselves, and opinions will differ about their success in solving it. They were, however, quite clear what the problem was, and they

[1] *Via Media: An essay in Theological Synthesis* (Longmans).
[2] The so-called 'Athanasian Creed', which, of course, is not by St Athanasius.

were determined to avoid, on the one hand the subordinationism which would make the Son and the Spirit God only in an honorary sense and, on the other, the modalism which would make them not really distinct from the Father.[1] They were also clear that something more was needed than the simple Aristotelian doctrine about the relation of individuals to their species, though they appear to have been less clear what 'it was. Dr Kelly has given an admirable summary of their thought in a passage which I will quote as a note at this point.[2] What strikes one is that, in spite of an initial reference to a universal and its particulars, they seem to have a clear grasp that

[1] Cf, e.g., the discussions of the Cappadocians in G. L. Prestige, *God in Patristic Thought* (SPCK, 2nd ed. 1952), chh. xi and xii; J. N. D. Kelly, *Early Christian Doctrines* (Black 1958), ch. x.

[2] 'To explain how the one substance can be simultaneously present in three Persons they appeal to the analogy of a universal and its particulars. "*Ousia* and *hypostasis*", writes Basil, "are differentiated exactly as universal (*koinon*) and particular (*to kath'hekaston*) are, e.g., animal and particular man." From this point of view each of the divine hypostases is the *ousia* or essence of the Godhead determined by its appropriate particularizing characteristic (*idiotēs*; *idiōma*), or identifying peculiarity (cf. *gnōristikai idiotētes*), just as each individual man represents the universal "man" determined by certain characteristics which mark him off from other men. For Basil these particularizing characteristics are respectively "paternity" (*patrotēs*), "sonship" (*huiotēs*), and "sanctifying power" or "sanctification" (*hagiastikē dunamis*; *hagiasmos*). The other Cappadocians define them more precisely as "ingenerateness" (*agennēsia*), "generateness" (*gennēsis*), and "mission" or "procession" (*ekpempsis*; *ekporeusis*), although Gregory of Nazianzus has to confess his inability to indicate wherein the Spirit's procession differs from the generation of the Son. Thus the distinction of the Persons is grounded in their origin and mutual relation. There are, we should observe, so many ways in which the one indivisible divine substance distributes and presents Itself, and hence they come to be termed "modes of coming to be" (*tropoi hyparxeōs*)' (Kelly, *Doctrines*, 265f).

the particularizing characteristics of the Persons are determined rather by the relations or comparisons of the Persons with one another – paternity, sonship, generation, mission – than by any proper and unshared characteristics of each; and it is this same sense that led Augustine to elaborate his notion of subsistent relations or relational being. It is most easily stated in terms of the first two Persons, in view of the elusiveness of the Spirit and of the lack of terms to denote him exclusively; so stated it means that all that distinguishes the Father and the Son from each other is that the Father possesses Godhead paternally and the Son filially, and that this involves eternal and complete self-giving by the Father and eternal and complete self-response by the Son. It must be emphasized that it is precisely because the self-giving of the Father is complete that it is the begetting of a co-equal Son and not the creation of an inferior creature; and it carries the implication that the glory of the Godhead consists not in an eternal self-possession but in an eternal self-giving.

St Augustine's adoption of the category of relation and his elevation of it to the level of substance is, of course, an example, perhaps the supreme example, of the use of analogy in theology,[1] and, like other uses, it has the limitation that, while the *perfectio significata* is familiar to us at the start, the *modus significandi* of its final application in the last resort eludes us.[2] But

[1] Cf. e.g., M. T.-L. Penido, *Le Rôle de l'Analogie en Théologie dogmatique* (Paris, Vrin, 1931), esp. 258ff.

[2] For this distinction, cf my *Existence and Analogy* (Longmans 1949) ch. v.

it has, I suggest, its uses and I believe that it is in fact a more valuable contribution to trinitarian theology than the 'psychological' analogies for which Augustine is famous. I believe that these, or at least that one which sees the begetting of the Son as analogous to the act of the intellect and the promission of the Spirit as analogous to the act of the will, is invaluable and virtually indispensable, but it needs the control of the relational analogy to keep it from distortion and aberration. It is important to observe in any case that Augustine's 'psychological' analogies fall into two quite distinct classes. The first, which he uses in a purely preliminary and introductory way and which, as Dr Kelly points out, many are quite wrong in assuming to be his principal trinitarian analogy,[1] is the analysis of the idea of love into the triad of the lover, the object loved and the love which unites them.[2] In Dr Kelly's words:

> His discussion of it is quite brief, and forms no more than a transition to what he considers his all-important analogy, based on the inner man, viz. the mind's activity as directed upon itself or, better still, upon God. This analogy fascinated him all his life, so that in such an early work as the *Confessions* (397–8) we find him pondering the triad of being, knowing and willing (*esse, nosse, velle*). In the *De Trinitate* he elaborates it at length in three successive stages, the resulting trinities being (a) the mind, its knowledge of itself, and its love of itself;[3] (b) memory or, more properly, the mind's latent knowlege

[1] *Doctrines*, 277.
[2] *De Trinitate*, IX, ii.
[3] *De Trinitate*, IX, iii–xii.

of itself, understanding, i.e. its apprehension of itself in the light of the eternal reasons, and the will, or love of itself, by which this process of self-knowledge is set in motion;[1] (c) the mind as remembering, knowing and loving God himself.[2] Each of these, in different degrees, reveals three real elements which, according to Augustine's metaphysic of personality, are coordinate and therefore equal, and at the same time essentially one; each of them throws light on the mutual relations of the divine Persons. It is the last of the three analogies, however, which Augustine deems most satisfactory.[3]

This analogy of the processions of the Son and the Spirit in the Godhead to the operations of intellect and will in the human mind became a commonplace in the theology of the West and in particular it received the weighty endorsement of St Thomas Aquinas in the thirteenth century. Thus he writes, with reference to 'actions that remain within the agent himself':

> In the spiritual world the only actions of this kind are those of the intellect and the will. But the Word's procession corresponds to the action of the intellect. Now in us there is another procession, which follows the action of the will, namely the procession of love, whereby what is loved is in the lover, just as in the conceiving of an idea the thing expressed or understood is in the knower. Thus besides the procession of the Word another procession is posited in the divinity, namely the procession of Love.[4]

It is, however, significant that, while St Thomas uses

[1] *De Trinitate*, X, viii–xii.
[2] *De Trinitate*, XIV, xii.
[3] *Doctrines*, 277f.
[4] *S. Theol.* I, xxvii, 3c.

the term 'real relations' to denote the personalizing characteristics of fatherhood, sonship, spiration and procession[1] and insists that what the Latins describe as 'person' is what the Greeks describe as *hypostasis*,[2] he is equally clear that what 'person' immediately signifies is *relation*:

> Divine person signifies relation as subsisting. And that is, to signify relation by the mode of substance which is a hypostasis subsisting in the divine nature.... In this sense it is true that the word 'person' signifies relation directly and essence indirectly; not however relation *as* relation, but in as far as it is signified in the mode of a hypostasis.[3]

It is fascinating to see the Angelic Doctor struggling to bring within the vocabulary of Aristotelianism this perplexing notion of a relation which has at the same time the character of a substance. He goes on to say, almost as if he was fearful of having gone too far:

> Likewise it [sc. person] signifies also essence directly and relation indirectly, inasmuch as essence is the same as hypostasis. In God, hypostasis signifies a distinct relation. And thus relation *as* relation indirectly falls under the idea of person.[4]

What Thomas is almost desperately concerned to exclude is the notion that there is, so to speak, a common property of 'personhood' which is common, uniformly and univocally, to Father, Son and Spirit

[1] ibid., xxviii, 4.
[2] ibid., xxix, 2c.
[3] ibid., xxix, 4c.
[4] ibid.

and to which the peculiar characteristic of each is an accidental addition. The point is in fact that there is *nothing* strictly common to the three persons except the fact of being God, of possessing the divine nature and enjoying the attributes that are identical with it. Thus neither substance nor relation *in its simple Aristotelian sense* measures up to the Christian understanding of Person. In Thomas's words: 'The problem about the meaning of 'person' [in God] arises because, unlike names referring to the essence, it is used of the three persons in the plural; nor does it refer to another, like words that signify a relation.'[1] But, he goes on to say, it *does* signify a relation, though one of a very special and unique kind:

> Distinction in God arises only through the relation of origin. However, a relation is in God not as an accident inhering in a subject, but it is the divine essence itself; therefore it is subsistent just as the divine essence subsists. So, just as Godhead is God, the divine Fatherhood is God the Father, who is a divine person. Hence 'divine person' signifies *a relation as subsisting*. This means a relation in the manner of a substance which is a hypostasis subsisting in the divine nature; though what is subsisting in the divine nature is just the divine nature itself.[2]

'A relation in the manner of a substance which is a hypostasis subsisting in the divine nature' – this is St Thomas's mature and considered understanding of 'person' as applied to Father, Son and Spirit, and it is of course from St Augustine that it is ultimately

[1] ibid., xxix, 4c.
[2] ibid.

derived. I have gone into this matter at some length, in spite of its technicality, because I hope it may be possible to mitigate the often expressed judgement that, from the time of Augustine onwards, Western theology has 'depersonalized the Deity'. This must be the subject of the next chapter.

II

Depersonalizing the Deity? – The Reaction of the East

In view of the clearly stated conviction of such loyal adherents of the Eastern tradition as Vladimir Lossky[1] and Dr John Meyendorff that, in the words of the latter, 'as long as the two schools of thoughts remained open to dialogue and mutual understanding, they could have developed in a complementary way',[2] I am sometimes tempted to wonder whether the alleged opposition between the two traditions may have been over-emphasized by such Western experts as Théodore de Régnon and Fr Karl Rahner. And the more I think about it the clearer it seems to me that, in so far as there was ever in the West a tendency to look on the one divine essence as primary and to see the three persons as simply differentiations within it, the great opponent of this was in fact Augustine, with his much maligned psychological analogies. For in all of these the second and third terms derive from the first, the mind's knowledge of itself and its love of itself, for example, both presupposing the mind as their origin in the first place. But, to repeat, I believe that Augustine's great contribution to trinitarian thinking was the view of the persons as subsistent relations. Dr Kelly has remarked that 'to modern people, unless

---

[1] Cf the passage quoted above on p. 14.

[2] *Byzantine Theology, historical trends and doctrinal themes* (Mowbray 1975), 181.

schooled in technical philosophy, the notion of relations ... as having a real subsistence sounds strange, although they are usually prepared to concede their objectivity, i.e. that they exist in their own right independent of the observer.'[1] For this reason there is, I think, much to be said for Fr Jean Galot's rendering 'relational being' (*être relationnel*),[2] to denote being whose status is constituted solely by its relatedness. In all their *attributes* – power, wisdom, goodness and the rest – Father, Son and Spirit are indistinguishable; what distinguishes them is simply their *relations* to one another, relations that establish the dependence of the Son and the Spirit on the Father.[3] Like everything else in God, these relations are not static but dynamic, and not schematic but constitutive. It is his active and total eternal self-expression and self-giving that constitutes the First Person as Father; it is his active and grateful response to its reception that constitutes the Second Person as Son.

It is almost impossible for us not to *imagine* the divine Persons as three individuals, each with his own different attributes; it is difficult for us to conceive of three subjects with identical attributes, whose distinction from one another consists only in the difference of their mutual relations. What, it may be asked in some exasperation, are you demanding of the

---

[1] *Doctrines*, 275.

[2] *La Personne du Christ*, 41f.

[3] Two cautions here:(1) I prescind at the moment from the issue of the *Filioque*; cf pp. 57ff infra. (2) I prescind also from the consideration of the Incarnation; the human nature of Jesus is hypostatically assumed by, and individuated in, the Person of the Son.

simple faithful under penalty of condemnation as heretics? Well, first of all, I am not demanding that the 'simple faithful' – and today this includes not only the equivalent of Pascal's 'charcoal-burner' but many literate and expensively educated people who have not had the opportunity or the inclination to indulge in philosophical and theological speculation – should put themselves under the discipline of Augustine, Aquinas, Lossky and Rahner, still less under mine. For them it will be enough to repeat with *Quicunque vult* that 'the Father is God, the Son God and the Holy Spirit God, and yet there are not three Gods but one God', and, if outraged intellectuals protest that such people must be self-condemned obscurantists, crypto-tritheists or unconscious Sabellians, the answer may simply be that, through participation in the tradition of Christian life and worship, they have come to experience God as he is. There is a knowledge by 'connaturality' through faith and love, which is more intimate then merely conceptual knowledge, and it is vital that intellectuals should remember this. Nevertheless, when intellectual issues are raised they must be faced, and it is disreputable for the intellectual to put on the mask of the charcoal-burner whenever he finds himself in a corner.

Secondly, it is important to recognize just what the recognition of God as tri-personal has done for the understanding of personality as such, with all that that has come to mean in terms of human individuality, rights and duties. Many have emphasized this; I will simply quote this passage from Lossky:

Our ideas of human personality, of that *personal* quality which makes every human being unique, to be expressed only in terms of itself: this idea of *person* comes to us from Christian theology. The philosophy of antiquity knew only human individuals. The human person cannot be expressed in concepts. It eludes all rational definitions, indeed all descriptions, for all the properties whereby it could be characterized can be met with in other individuals. Personality can only be grasped in this life by a direct intuition; it can only be expressed in a work of art.... And yet human persons, or hypostases, are isolated and, in the words of St John Damascene, 'do not exist the one within the other'; while, 'in the Holy Trinity it is quite the reverse ... the hypostases dwell in one another'.... Indeed, each of the three hypostases contains the unity, the one nature, after the manner proper to it, and which, in distinguishing it from the other two persons, recalls at the same time the indissoluble bond uniting the Three.[1]

What is lacking here is any clear indication of the character of this feature, which distinguishes persons but can be grasped only by intuition and which, we are told intriguingly, 'can only be expressed in a work of art'. Fr Galot, in his brilliant extension of Augustine's insight from trinitarian theology into Christology,[2] has identified the missing factor with Augustine's notion of substantial relation. Starting from the generally accepted point that 'person' stands for that element or aspect of a rational being that is essentially

---

[1] *Mystical Theology* ..., 53f.
[2] *Personne* ..., 27ff et passim. I have discussed Galot's Christology at length in *Theology and the Gospel of Christ*, 151ff.

incommunicable,[1] he widens it with the notion of *community*; and this, he stresses, is basically *relational*:

> Human persons ... do not first of all exist in their separate self-enclosures, to enter later on into relation with others and form a community with them. Community and person are posited together; a person only exists as a relation with other persons. Its reality is that of a relational being. An ego has meaning only in its relation with other egos.[2]

This balanced duality in the person, Galot insists, is manifested perfectly and fully only in God himself; in creatures it is a genuine but partial analogue of what it is in God, and Galot is at pains to elucidate wherein that partiality consists. That is not our present concern; it will, however, be relevant to see how he envisages it in God:

> The mystery of the Trinity is presented as the sharpest denial of any individualistic personalism; it is the most impressive witness to the communitary aspect of the person. It indicates notably that in God the persons are not constituted antecedently to their community, as if they formed wholes in themselves before opening themselves to the others. They are constituted in their mutual relations, the ego of the Father being posited only as his relation to the ego of the Son and being united to him in the ego of the Holy Spirit.... Community

---

[1] Even if the names were removed from their collars, Tweedledum and Tweedledee would still be two persons and not one.

[2] op. cit, 43. Essentially the same point is made by the Greek Orthodox scholar Dr John D. Zizioulas in his difficult but rewarding work *Being as Communion* (Darton 1985), with its subtitle 'Studies in Personhood and the Church'.

is not *posterior* to the persons; it is established simultaneously with them.[1]

We are not concerned here with Galot's penetrating analysis of the difference between the ways in which the notion of relational being applies to the uncreated Persons of the Godhead and to created human persons, or to his use of it in Christology; I have discussed both of these elsewhere.[2] The following passages, however, are directly relevant, for their reference to the *equality* of the Persons:

> The notion of relational being is most apt to designate the specific relation which unites one person to others. It properly applies to the interpersonal relation. It does not imply the inferiority of one ego with regard to another ego, for the level of an interpersonal relation is rather that of equality.
>
> If it implied dependence, it is a mutal dependence that characterizes the situation with regard to other egos. For interpersonal relation is always reciprocal. It differs in this from relativity in the natural order, where dependence can be unilateral; the creature depends on the Creator and not *vice versa*....
>
> Let us insist on the fact that, in speaking of a relational being, we do not envisage a being which becomes relational by appropriating relations but a being which has no reality other than being relational.... The relation does not only 'enter' into being of the ego; it essentially forms it.[3]

What, then, can we say about the three Persons

[1] ibid., 42, my italics.
[2] *Theology and the Gospel of Christ*, 153ff, 157ff.
[3] *Personne* ..., 43f. I am responsible for rendering *moi* by 'ego'.

severally, if we are to describe them in purely relational terms? Only, it would seem, that they are God-begetting, God-begotten, God-proceeding, for to say anything more, even to attempt to describe what begetting and procession are, would appear to involve us in ascribing to one of the Persons exclusively some attribute that belongs to the Godhead as such. The Father is Love, perhaps you say. But then are not the Son and the Spirit Love as well? The apostolic writer simply tells us that *God* is Love, without qualification.[1] Well, then, you reply, let us distinguish the three as Love begetting, Love begotten and Love proceeding. But now, I object, we are back where we started; what do 'begetting' and 'proceeding' mean, in purely relational terms, when applied to Love or anything else? Has Augustine's clever device merely left us chasing our own tails in a ballet of bloodless abstractions?

Not, I think, if we remember whence we derive our knowledge that God is Trinity in any case, namely the assumption of human nature – our nature – by the Son. 'No man has seen God at any time;' declares the Gospel, 'the only-begotten Son, who is in the bosom of the Father, he has declared him.'[2] In technical theological terms, this means that it is not just God that we see incarnate in Jesus, but *God-the-Son*; not just the undifferentiated self-existent Supreme Being of natural theology, but deity responding filially to

[1] I John iv. 8.

[2] John i. 18. There is an impressive variant, preferred by the weighty Nestle/Kilpatrick text, 'the only-begotten God'.

deity communicated paternally and taking human nature into its filial response. It is the recognition of this truth that is the strength of the work on Christology of Fr. Louis Bouyer and of that of Fr Jean Galot, and that has enabled them to contribute constructively to the problem that has so deeply concerned modern writers, that of the content of the human consciousness of the incarnate Son; I have discussed it at length elsewhere.[1] It is, also, I think, the basis of Fr Karl Rahner's frequent insistence that the 'economic' and the 'immanent' Trinity are identical and that it is not a mere 'accident' that it is the Son and not the Father or the Spirit that has become incarnate. If we wish to understand, however partially, what is involved in a Fatherhood and a Sonship that are purely relational, we shall, I suggest, do well, whether we are 'charcoal-burners' or professional intellectuals, to study not merely the tortuosities of Karl Rahner and the profundities of Jean Galot, nor even the unembroidered formulas of *Quicunque vult*, but the words of the Gospel, in which we see, manifested in a human consciousness and expressed in human language, the self-articulation of filial deity. And, in those glimpses of his intercourse with the Father which the Gospels give us, what we see is not a formalized consciousness of his own deity (as if Jesus was constantly calling to mind the fact that he is God), nor even a *formalized* consciousness of his own sonship (as if he was constantly calling to mind the fact that he is the unique and eternal Son), but rather the fullest consciousness of God as the

[1] *Theology and the Gospel of Christ*, ch. iii.

Father who eternally begets him in a unique act of totally complete self-giving and evokes from him an equally total filial response. That he has an *unthematized* awareness (to use Rahner's phrase) of his own divinity goes without saying, and it rises to the thematic or formalized level on occasion, when he speaks to his hearers with the authority of God, as the Son who is invested with his Father's authority; but when he speaks to the Father it is always as the Son, totally submissive and receptive. In Père Bouyer's words, 'Jesus was "the Christ, the Son of the living God", not directly by knowing that he was, but because he knew God *as the Father*, with everything of the unique and the ineffable that that means for him according to the Gospel.'[1] And the point which I wish to make here is that this filial relation which we see on the created level in the human life of Jesus is simply the incarnation of the filial relation which, on the uncreated level, is the filiality of the eternally begotten Son. On the created level it is, of course, the homage of an inferior to a superior, though it is a homage which is entirely willing, joyful and grateful; Jesus is, as the *Quicunque vult* reminds us, 'less than the Father in respect of his humanity'. But he is, according to the same authority, 'equal to the Father in respect of his divinity'; and one of the surprising things that the Incarnation teaches us is that *dependence*, even that ultimate and total dependence involved in the reception by one person

---

[1] *Le Fils éternel* (Paris, Cerf, 1974), 510. For the Christological aspects of this cf my *Theology and the Gospel of Christ*, 137, 162; *Whatever happened to the Human Mind?*, 53ff.

of his very existence from another, does not necessarily involve inferiority.[1] Indeed, it might be said that it is *especially* in the reception of his very existence by the Son from the Father that dependence does not involve inferiority, since what the Father communicates to the Son in eternally begetting him is nothing less than the fullness of his own being. And I think it is by emphasizing the completeness of the Father's giving of himself that we can see that the difference between the two Persons consists, not in any difference in their several natures (for each possesses the one nature of God), but simply in their mutual and reciprocal relatedness, it being equally stressed that this relatedness is not a merely logical or schematic comparability but a metaphysical and existential reality. The Persons are not just relations, but *substantial* relations; in Galot's term, they are *relational being*.

---

[1] Cf the discussion of the notion of 'derived equality' in my *Via Media*, 47ff.

III

The Anonymous Spirit

Hitherto I have said almost nothing about the Third Person of the Trinity, and the reader might perhaps wonder whether, like the disciples of John the Baptist whom St Paul found at Ephesus,[1] I had never so much as heard that there was a Holy Spirit. I shall in fact have a good deal to say about the Holy Spirit later on, but I have two other excuses for the line that I have followed. First, that I have been concerned to defend and interpret the notion of person as relational being, and the relation of the Father and the Son was the obvious starting-point. But, secondly, that there is a peculiar elusiveness about the Spirit which demands a special consideration; and to that I shall now turn.

Even the name – 'Holy Spirit' – by which the Third Person of the Godhead is known witnesses to this elusiveness, for it is one that might fittingly apply to the other Persons as well. Augustine indeed argues that because 'he is common to both he has as proper what they have in common',[2] and St Thomas, quoting this, stresses that 'the Father is spirit, the Son spirit; the Father is holy, the Son holy',[3] but this is rather an argument of 'convenience' than a knock-down proof. And St John gives even higher authority for the

[1] Acts xix, 2.
[2] *De Trinitate*, XV, xix.
[3] *S. Theol.* I, xxvi, 1c.

simple assertion that 'God is spirit'.[1] Furthermore, although the Eastern and Western churches have been to this day in vigorous opposition as to the source within the Trinity from which the Third Person proceeds, their theologians are agreed on the difficulty of finding a word to to denote his particular mode of procession. Thus St Thomas, even after he has distinguished the processions of the Son and the Spirit as analogous to the intellect and the will respectively, has to admit that, while there are compulsive grounds for denoting the former as 'generation' or 'begetting', 'the procession which is not generation has remained without a special name'; and he takes refuge in the tautological reflection that 'it can be called "spiration", since it is the procession of the Spirit'.[2] St John of Damascus, who has been called 'the Aquinas of the East', writes: 'We have learned that there is a difference between generation and procession, but the nature of the difference we in no wise understand'.[3] And Lossky, in the heart of the Orthodox tradition:

> We reach a paradoxical conclusion; all that we know of the Spirit refers to his economy [i.e., his dealing with creatures]; all that we do not know makes us venerate his person, as we venerate the ineffable diversity of the consubstantial Three.[4]

There is a further reason for the 'anonymity' of

[1] John iv, 24.
[2] *S. Theol.* I, xxvii, 4 ad 3.
[3] *De Fide Orth.*, P.G. XCIV, 824A, cit. Lossky, *Mystical Theology ...*, 55.
[4] V. Lossky, *In the Image and Likeness of God* (Mowbrays 1975), 75.

the Spirit, based on the divine 'economy'; it arises ultimately from the ordered relationship (the *taxis*, as the Greeks say) of the three Persons in the Trinity. The Father, although totally unknowable to us by himself, is revealed to us by the Son, who is his perfect image and has assumed our human nature: 'No man has seen God at any time; the only begotten Son, who is in the bosom of the Father, he has declared him.'[1] But that Jesus himself is Lord can be recognized only through the Holy Spirit,[2] whose 'economy' within the Church is to be the interpreter of the Son.[3] 'One does not think of the Father without the Son;' writes St Gregory of Nyssa, 'one does not conceive of the Son without the Holy Spirit. For it is impossible to attain to the Father except by being raised by the Son, and it is impossible to call Jesus Lord save in the Holy Spirit.'[4] There is, however, no fourth Person in the Godhead to reveal or interpret the Spirit. He is necessarily the interpreter rather than the interpreted. Lossky has made this point clearly and constructively, illustrating it by a number of passages from the Eastern fathers:

> The third Hypostasis of the Trinity is the only one not having his image in another Person. The Holy Spirit, as Person, remains unmanifested, hidden, concealing himself in his very appearing.... The doctrine of the Holy Spirit (in contrast to the dazzling manifestation of the Son which the Church proclaims to the farthest

[1] John i, 18.
[2] I Cor. xii, 3.
[3] John. xiv, 26.
[4] P.G. XLIV, 1316, cit. Lossky, *Mystical Theology* ..., 160.

confines of the universe), has the character of a secret, a partially revealed tradition.... We confess the Holy Trinity. But the very Person of the Holy Spirit who reveals these truths to us and who renders them inwardly luminous, manifest, almost tangible to us, nevertheless remains himself undisclosed and hidden, concealed by the deity which he reveals to us, by the gift which he imparts.[1]

In view of this 'anonymity' of the Spirit, I do not think we should be much concerned by the smallness of the place which the Spirit has received *quantitatively* in the official liturgical worship of the Church. There are indeed a few hymns of beauty, sobriety and dogmatic precision addressed directly to the Spirit in the Latin liturgy, such as the *Veni Creator Spiritus*, the office-hymn for Terce *Nunc Sancte nobis Spiritus*, and the 'Golden Sequence' *Veni Sancte Spiritus*.[2] There is also, in the Byzantine rite, the brief but lovely prayer 'O heavenly King, the Comforter',[3] which is not only part of the preparation in the Liturgy and the Offices but is a normal element in the daily devotions of the Orthodox laity. Such formularies, in which the Spirit is directly addressed, are however very rare in both East and West. This should not, in my opinion, be a matter for anxiety, provided – and this is essential – that the correct trinitarian structure of worship is maintained. If, with a well-meaning but wrong-headed desire of restoring to the Spirit the recognition of which it is felt that he has been deprived, devotion is

[1] *Mystical Theology* ..., 160ff.
[2] Translations, E.H. 154, 255, 155.
[3] E.H. 454 is a free verse-translation.

improvised that is directly focussed on him in detachment from the other two Persons, two dangers immediately appear. The first is that, because of the 'anonymity' of the Spirit, such devotion can only too easily become uncontrolled and independent of the life of the Church as a whole; the second is that, for the same reason, other spirits of very dubious character may successfully impersonate the true Spirit and lead those whom they deceive into situations of the gravest danger. St Paul's epistles bear witness to the fact that times of great outpouring of the Spirit are also times when the discernment of the spirits is of supreme importance.

Thus, what might be described as the normal or natural pattern of Christian prayer is directed *to* the Father *through* the Son and *in* the Spirit, but this without any suggestion that the Son and the Spirit are inferior to the Father. The liturgical expression of the notion of derived equality was not achieved by the Church without difficulty and dispute. The great Liturgical scholar Josef Jungmann has described how the doxological form 'Glory to the Father through the Son and in the Holy Spirit', which was in general use in the fourth century, was seized upon by Arian and Macedonian heretics as implying that the Son and the Spirit were inferior to the Father, and how the orthodox in reaction replaced it by the form 'Glory to the Father and to the Son and to the Holy Spirit' (*Gloria Patri et Filio et Spiritui Sancto*) or 'Glory to the Father with the Son together with the Holy Spirit' (*Doxa tō Patri meta tou Huiou sun Hagio Pneumati*).

> In the older formula [Jungmann writes], prominence is given to the voluntary abasement by which the Son descended down to us, becoming our Saviour and Shepherd; therefore we can pray *through* him. And in it, too, the Holy Spirit is pictured, so to say, as the place where we can adore God; therefore we can pray *in* him. The new formula, on the other hand, expresses rather the adoration we owe equally to the Father and to the Son and to the Holy Spirit; and it harmonises with the words with which we are baptised, 'in the name of the Father and of the Son and of the Holy Spirit'.[1]

Jungmann gives other examples of the way in which the victory over Arian and Macedonian heresy, necessary as it was, was accompanied by losses in the realm of liturgical expression and theological subtlety. Our present concern is with the fact that insistence on the equality of the three Persons has led (at any rate in the formulas of worship) to a neglect of their mutual relations. And it is then only a short step to the view of some of the medievals that, if there was to be an Incarnation, it would have been just as fitting for the Father or the Spirit to have become man as for the Son.

We may at least agree with Jungmann that 'the struggle with heresy, though ultimately victorious, yet led in many points to losses', though his further remark that 'the conflict left its mark not only on the liturgy, especially in the East, but also on the peculiar character of oriental piety'[2] might be supplemented by the qualification that the West has not been left

---

[1] *The Early Liturgy* (Darton 1960), 193f.
[2] ibid., 198.

entirely unaffected either. And I would suggest that the basic reason for the distortion and imbalance which have affected Christian spirituality in both East and West and which have left their mark on the expressions and accompaniments, if not on the essence, of the liturgy itself, is not that the deity of Jesus has been stressed to the neglect of his humanity, but that he has been thought of simply as God rather than as God-the-Son. The truth is not simply that in Jesus one of the divine Persons has become man, never mind which, but that God-the-Son has become man and that in him manhood has been made filial to the Eternal Father. In consequence those who have been adopted into Jesus have been made filial to the Father in Him.[1] (Whether it was metaphysically possible, even if less fitting, for the Father or the Spirit rather than the Son to have become man, is one of those questions that may perhaps be validly described as academic.[2]) Thus, *To* the Father, *through* the Son, *in* the Spirit becomes not only the pattern of Christian prayer but also the pattern of Christian living. And, precisely because he is God and is God-the-Son there is really no contradiction between worship of Jesus and worship of the Father. When Bishop Polycarp was called upon to renounce Christ in the stadium at Smyrna and replied 'I have been his servant for eighty-six years and he has never done me any wrong. How then can I blaspheme my king who saved me?', he did not need to take precautions that his allegiance was compatible

[1] Gal. iv, 4ff.
[2] Cf St Thomas Aquinas, *S. Theol.* III, iii, 5 et 8.

with strict monotheism. And even when, in the West, the Eucharist seemed to have become for many people simply a service of adoration of Jesus present in the sacred Host, the Host itself had been consecrated by the prayer addressed to the Father through the Son in the unity of the Holy Spirit. The Roman Church never found it necessary, in maintaining its trinitarian orthodoxy, to adopt, as the Byzantines did, the violent expedient of suddenly changing the Eucharistic prayer, in its final clause, from being a prayer to the Father to being a glorification of the Trinity. The normal ending of formal prayer in the West – 'through Jesus Christ thy Son our Lord, who liveth and reigneth with thee in the unity of the Holy Spirit God for ever and ever', *ad Patrem per Filium in Spiritu*, expresses the Church's consciousness that when she approaches the Father she is caught up into the filial response which the Son himself makes in the life of the Godhead, filial yet none the less divine. We may nevertheless note that the accepted doxological formula 'Glory to the Father and to the Son and to the Holy Spirit', while it expresses succinctly and uncompromisingly the absolute equality of the three divine Persons, fails altogether to indicate the particular characteristics of each or the relations between them. Indeed, it is only by implication (in ascribing the one glory to all three) that it affirms the basic belief of monotheism that they are one God and not three gods.

Dr T. F. Torrance, whose admiration of St Athanasius is extreme among Protestant theologians, has claimed to discern a certain deviation in later Greek trinitarian thought.

> The Athanasian doctrine of God [he writes] has to be distinguished somewhat from that which came to prevail in later Greek thought through the Cappadocian stress upon the idea that the Father alone is the *archē*, *pēgē*, or *aitia*, i.e. source or principle, fount or cause of Godhead, together with the tendency to distinguish the divine *energeiai* from the divine *ousia*. That way of thinking implied that while the Deity of the Son and the Deity of the Spirit are co-eternal and co-equal with the Deity of the Father, for there is only one Godhead, nevertheless the Son and the Spirit have a *derived* Deity, while that of the Father is *underived* Deity. That is particularly evident in the teaching of John of Damascus. In contrast, as we have seen, for Athanasius the 'whole Godhead' is complete in the Son and in the Spirit as much as it is in the Father. God is God the Son as much as he is God the Father, and the Son of God is God precisely as the Father is God, for each is whole and proper to the other, so that *the same things are said of each except that one is called Father and the other Son*. Thus while the Son is certainly *of* the Father he is not thought of as derived or caused, for he is Son *of* the Father as the Father is Father *of* the Son; thus the *of* belongs to the full mutuality of the Father and of the Son within the one unchangeable Being of the one God, without any kind of superiority or inferiority being implied, even though it is denied in the same breath.[1]

I cannot here discuss in detail Dr Torrance's account of St Athanasius's trinitarian teaching or assess his

---
[1] *Theology in Reconciliation* (Geoffrey Chapman 1975), 252 (italics in original).

claim that the great Alexandrian doctor was faced with essentially the same problems that confront us today and provides us with the guide-lines that we ourselves need. I am sure that any modern Eastern Orthodox theologian will maintain that the Cappadocian insight that Deity can be derived without being devalued is not a contradiction of the Athanasian doctrine but a deepening and a development of it, and on this I would agree. I would add that this is not to belittle Athanasius's stature but to exalt it. (And if it is supposed that this is a purely academic question without any possible practical implications, I would point to the bearing which various Orthodox theologians, notably Dr Thomas Hopko,[1] have shown it to have on the burning question of the ordination of women to the priesthood.) I have given a brief sketch of the subsequent history of this insight in the chapter of my book *Via Media* which I have already mentioned. And it cannot be too strongly emphasized that what was involved was not a philosophical exercise in the handling of logical concepts but the Church's ongoing struggle to articulate in human speech the Truth that had become incarnate in Christ and was the heart of her own experience and existence as his Body.

---

[1] *Women and the Priesthood*, ed. Thomas Hopko (Crestwood, N.Y., St Vladimir's Seminary Press 1983), esp. 134–190.

IV

The Trinity and the World

It has been a firmly held principle of Western theology, given dogmatic status by the Council of Florence in 1442, that 'in God everything is one where there is no relational contrast' ([*in Deo*] *omnia sunt unum ubi non obviat relationis oppositio*),[1] and this is often expanded in the form that 'all the acts of God to the exterior are acts of the one God and not of particular Persons'. This was of course motivated by the extreme concern of theologians to insist on the unity of God against all forms of polytheism. It is not contradicted by the affirmations of Scripture about the Son that 'all things were created through him and for him'[2] and that he 'upholds the universe by his word of power'[3] – affirmations also reflected in the Creeds – for it is clear that his exercise of this creative function is altogether within his filial relation to the Father. Nor is it contradicted by the fact that it is the Second Person of the Trinity, and not the First or the Third, who has become man, for, if person is *relational being*, the Incarnation is certainly *not* a case 'where there is no relational contrast'. But we may go farther than this and hold with Karl Rahner that, although it is the Son who has become the personal (hypostatic) subject

[1] DS 1330.
[2] Col. i, 16.
[3] Heb. i, 3.

of the human nature of Jesus of Nazareth, nevertheless the Incarnation, if considered in its widest aspect, must be seen as one inclusive activity of the triune God, in which each of the Persons is involved in the way proper to his own relational character.[1] Thus the Father's preordination and the Spirit's overshadowing of Mary are no less integral to the Incarnation than is the assumption of human nature by the Son. In St Luke's account of the Annunciation the angel's message gives equal place and relevance to the Son and the Spirit. We are far from the view which has been described as holding that it was a toss-up which of the three Persons should become man and that when the Son had won the toss neither of the other two was involved any more.[2]

Beyond these evidently relational attributions there are others which Christian writers have allocated to the several divine Persons which are more difficult to justify. St Thomas quotes Hilary as associating eternity with the Father, image and beauty with the Son, and gift and joy (*usus*) with the Spirit. Then he takes three triads from Augustine: (1) unity, equality, and the conjunction of the two; (2) might, wisdom, and goodness; and (3) the threefold phrase of St Paul in Romans xi, 36 'from him, and through him, and in him.' The difficulty here – and it requires all the Angelic Doctor's ingenuity to cope with it[3] – is that,

[1] *The Trinity* (Burns & Oates 1970), 86ff.
[2] It should be made plain that St Thomas's view was much more subtle than this (*S. Theol.* III, iii, 5–8; iv, 1.) Cf my *Whatever happened ...*, 129.
[3] *S. Theol.* I, xxxix, 7, 8.

although all the epithets apply appropriately to God (provided allowance is made for the radically analogous character of all human language in this context), it is difficult in most cases to argue convincingly that any one of them applies more appropriately to one of the divine Persons than to another. The doctrine of 'appropriation', on the basis of which it is held that terms that apply to the Godhead as such can be legitimately applied to one Person rather than to another, would seem to require more careful argument in its support than it has sometimes received, if it is to be reconciled with the principle which has been so strongly emphasized in the West, that all God's acts *ad extra* are acts of the one God. The Orthodox may perhaps have a valid point when they criticize the Latins for having divided their discussions of God into two sharply delimited treatises: *De Deo uno*, concerned with natural theology, and *De Deo Trino*, concerned with revelation. Is not creation, they protest indignantly, no less than redemption, the work of the triune God? The point is a sound one; nevertheless, it may be replied, many serious thinkers who are not Christians have come to believe in a supreme and self-existent Deity who is the creator of the universe; St Paul remarked on this,[1] and many sets of Gifford Lectures witness to it. And it should be possible, whether we are concerned with God's activity in nature or in grace, to hold that it is the One God who is acting and at the same time to admit that, within this one activity, each of the Persons is involved in

[1] Romans i, 20.

his particular relational capacity, whether in any specific case, this trinitarian character is overt and manifest or, so to speak, implicit and incognito.

Karl Rahner has remarked that the sharp distinction between the treatises *De Deo Uno* and *De Deo Trino* came into general use only in the thirteenth century, when the *Sententiae* of Peter Lombard were replaced by the *Summa* of St Thomas as a theological handbook.[1] His suggestion that its ultimate source may be St Augustine may be debatable, but his account of the outlook it embodies is important

> Here [he writes] in contrast to the Greeks, one begins with the one single nature of God as a totality, and only considers him *after that* as constituted by three persons – though this involves a constant (and necessary) effort to avoid posing the '*essentia*' as a 'fourth element' previous to the three persons. It would be more Biblical and Greek to start from the one absolutely unoriginated God, who is still the Father, even when it is not yet known that he is the Begetter and Spirator, because he is known as the unoriginated hypostasis, even when he is not yet known expressly as relative. But the starting-point of the Latins in the Middle Ages was different. And so it is possible to think that the Christian treatise *De Deo Uno* can and should be placed *before De Deo Trino*. But then one really writes, or could merely write, a treatise '*De Divinitate una*', since the unicity of the divine being justifies this procedure, and make it very philosophical and abstract in development – which is of course what happens – with very little concrete reference to the history of salvation....

[1] *Theological Investigations* (Darton 1966), IV, 83.

'But then,' Rahner adds, referring to the situation thus produced,

> the theology of the Trinity cannot but give the impression of being able to make merely formal assertions about the divine persons, with the help of the notions of the two processions and the relations. And even these assertions seem to deal with a reality entirely centred on itself, a Trinity which is not opened to anything outside, and of which we, the outsiders, only know something through a strange paradox.[1]

With his customary fairness he makes the admission:

> It must however be conceded here that when Greek theology was most flourishing, among the Cappadocian Fathers, it seems to have been almost more formalistic than the theology of the Trinity in St Augustine – in spite of a starting-point for the doctrine of the Trinity which was taken from the economy of salvation and was directed towards the world.

And he makes the suggestion:

> Should we not therefore say that the West took over the formal portion of the theology of the Trinity from the Greeks and made it *the* (whole) doctrine of the Trinity – since its soteriology [i.e. its doctrine of salvation] retains only the dogmatically unavoidable minimum of the theology of the Trinity?

And he asks, still more speculatively:

> Is not this why western theologians were forced – in contrast to the Greeks – to fill out this almost mathematical and formalistic theology by giving it more substance

[1] ibid., 84.

and content from the 'psychological' doctrine of the Trinity as developed by St Augustine?[1]

I will not attempt a detailed discussion of the 'Remarks on the Dogmatic Treatise "De Trinitate"' from which these passages are taken. I will only remark that even those Western theologians who were most committed to the principle that all the acts of God *ad extra* are acts of the one undivided deity have been unhappy at the suggestion that revelation has no light to cast upon the act of creation and the nature of createdness. St Thomas himself, after citing Dionysius the Psuedo-Areopagite to the effect that 'all that is causal is common to the whole divinity', qualified this by saying that 'the divine Persons have causality with respect to the creation of things according to the character of their processions.' 'God,' he continues, 'is the cause of things through his intellect and will, as an artist is of his works of art.... Thus God the Father wrought the creature through his Word, who is the Son, and through his Love, who is the Holy Spirit.' In rational creatures we find an image of the Trinity, but in all creatures a 'trace' (*vestigium*); each is a 'likeness' (*repraesentatio*).[2] In 1944 Père Lucien Chambat made the novel suggestion that the Dionysian principle applies only in the order of efficient causality, and that in the order of exemplary causality creation is an extension into the finite realm

---

[1] ibid., 85n.
[2] *S. Theol.* I, xlv, 6, 7.

of the eternal processions of the divine Persons.[1] But in 1941 Dorothy L. Sayers, who had already made a reputation as a novelist and dramatist, as well as a brilliant Christian apologist, gave a striking exposition of the doctrine of the Trinity by developing in her own way St Thomas's figure of God as the Creative Artist. In the book which she entitled *The Mind of the Maker*[2] she gave expression to the conviction, which she derived from her own experience as both a writer and a critic, that the creative act consists of three stages, and that these stages correspond with the three Persons of the Godhead, of whose supreme creative activity all human creative activity is a partial reflection. She had stated her thesis, precisely and dramatically, several years earlier, in a speech put into the mouth of the Archangel Michael:

> Praise Him that He hath made man in His own image, a maker and craftsman like himself, a little mirror of His triune majesty.
>
> For every work of creation is threefold, an earthly trinity to match the heavenly.
>
> First: there is the Creative Idea; passionless, timeless, beholding the whole work complete at once, the end in the beginning; and this is the image of the Father.
>
> Second: there is the Creative Energy, begotten of that Idea, working in time from the beginning to the end, with sweat and passion, being incarnate in the bonds of matter; and this is the image of the Word.
>
> Third: there is the Creative Power, the meaning of the

---

[1] *Présence et Union: Les Missions des Personnes de la Sainte-Trinité* (Paris, Fontenelle). K. Rahner appeared to hold this view, at least on the level of grace: *Theological Investigations* (Darton 1961), I, 334ff.

[2] Methuen.

work and its response in the lively soul; and this is the image of the Indwelling Spirit. And these three are one, each equally in itself the whole work, whereof none can exist without the other; and this is the image of the Trinity.[1]

Opinions will no doubt differ about Miss Sayers's handling of her theme, and there are questions which she left unanswered. Are we to see human creative activity simply as an analogue of God's creative activity, or are we in addition to see the latter as itself an analogue of the inner trinitarian life of God himself? Is the supreme and archetypal artistic activity that by which the Father eternally begets the Son and promits the Spirit? Of one thing we can be sure, that Dorothy Sayers would have vigorously repudiated any suggestion that she had discovered some novel and hitherto unsuspected truths about God; she was always emphatic that in all her apologetic work she was simply expounding truths – often forgotten or misunderstood truths – that were part of the deposit of faith. She was clear that human creativity needs to be controlled by Christian truth, and not *vice versa*; and, as her biographer Mr James Brabazon points out, she went so far as to attribute particular literary and artistic defects to specific imbalances in trinitarian doctrine:

> Part of the delight of the book [he writes, with reference to *The Mind of the Maker*] is the way in which Dorothy works out the details of this imaginative idea. She discusses, in terms of actual works of art, what happens

[1] *The Zeal of Thy House*, Play for Canterbury Cathedral (Gollancz 1937), cit. James Brabazon, *Dorothy L. Sayers* (Gollancz 1981), 206.

when one or other of the three persons of the Trinity is stronger or weaker than others. In some writers or artists, for example, it is obvious that the original idea was a noble and powerful one, but the technique is insufficient to convey it. In others, the technique is flawless but they have nothing much to say. There are yet others – sentimental popular writers, for example, who have neither anything much to say nor any particular skill in saying it, but who have a special knack of communicating with large numbers of people on a superficial level. Here the Spirit is more powerful than either Father or Son.

These imbalances correspond to the heresies of Christianity, all of which are cases of an over-emphasis on one or other aspect of Christian truth at the expense of others; the Church's job being to hold the balance right.'[1]

Two years after Miss Sayers' book appeared I was brave enough to make, in my first substantial work,[2] some elaborations of St Thomas's teaching about the *vestigium*, though my own background was not that of art and literature but of mathematics and natural science. These were the declining years of the great age of natural theology and the mighty Gifford Lecturers, whose sequence had included James Ward, Pringle-Pattison, Balfour, Alexander, Inge, C. C. J. Webb, von Hügel, A. E. Taylor, Whitehead and William Temple. Only by exception did they include a Thomist like Etienne Gilson or an avowed opponent of natural theology like Karl Barth. Solidly based upon Kant, with occasional leanings to Hegel, they defended a

[1] Brabazon, op. cit., 207.
[2] *He Who Is: A Study in Traditional Theism* (Longmans 1943, 2nd ed., Darton 1966).

God who might be limited, dependent or even evolving, but who did at any rate exist; not from their lips did the Scottish universities hear about the logical and linguistic atheism of Vienna and Oxford. And, having given a critique of the Cosmology of A. N. Whitehead and the Cosmic Teleology of F. R. Tennant, I thought it might be useful to make a brief discussion of the relation between natural theology and the doctrine of the Trinity. Starting from St Thomas's assertion that, although to create is not proper to any one Person but is common to the whole Trinity, there is nevertheless found a trace (*vestigium*) of the Trinity in all creatures, I went on to enquire whether modern cosmology can help us to understand wherein this trace consists. And here I made what I was careful to describe as 'some very tentative suggestions'.

> There are in the world [I wrote] two great contrasts which force themselves on our attention. The first is the contrast between the actual and the possible; the second the contrast between permanence and change.[1]

I went on to point out that the common assumption of nineteenth-century physicists that the world could be taken as a self-obvious axiomatic fact had collapsed with the materialism on which it depended and that A. S. Eddington's attempt to show on metrological principles (that is, by consideration of the operation of *measurement* alone) that the world is logically inevitable was generally rejected as unconvincing. Whitehead's distinction between the 'eternal objects' and the 'actual

[1] op. cit., 187.

occasions' into which they are ingredient had the merit of emphasizing the contrast between possibility and actuality, in spite of the weakness of his basic immanentism as an ultimate metaphysical explanation of the world's existence. And these two contrasts, I claimed, between the actual and the possible and between permanence and change, presented us with three irreducible and mutually implicated facts of experience which could be summarized as follows:

(i) There is an infinite realm of abstract possibility.
(ii) There is, selected from this realm, a limited realm of actual concrete occurrence.
(iii) In contrast with the former realm, there is in this latter realm a process of change.

And I suggested that 'these three facts are to be correlated (in Thomist language, 'appropriated') to the three Persons of the Trinity, as, in virtue of their mutual coinherence, they all concur in the unity of the creative act.'[1] I must refer to my text for the arguments by which I supported this identification; they still seem to me to be plausible, though I am not quite so confident about this as I was. What it is quite essential to make plain when experimenting with this or any other analogy for the part played by the divine Persons in the creative act is that we are concerned with three factors or elements within the one act and not with three acts, one for each of the Persons. Any weakening on this point is a virtual concession to tritheism. Here we have both Scripture and tradition

[1] ibid., 188.

on our side. In the New Testament, 'God' (*ho theos*) *tout simplement* is the Father, the Maker of heaven and earth.[1] But from all eternity he has begotten a Son, who is the effulgence of his glory and the very image of his substance,[2] very God from very God. And so when he creates a world, which is itself a finite copy of his own infinite splendour, the creative act is itself a finite copy of the begetting of the Son. So, *in* the Son, who is the image of the invisible God, all things were created, in heaven and on earth;[3] *through* the Son the Father made the worlds.[4] 'To us there is one God the Father, *from* whom are all things and we *unto* him; and one Lord Jesus Christ, *through* whom are all things and we *through* him.[5] Therefore, not only is the creation of the world *through* the Son a finite analogue of the begetting of the Son by the Father, but also its creation *in* him gives it a participation in the filial response which the Son makes to the Father. And all this is under the overshadowing of the Spirit, who is the Lord and the Giver of life. If we firmly grasp that all God's acts *ad extra* are acts of the One God and are at the same time acts of the Trinity – because there is only one God and he is the Trinity – and that in all these acts each of the Persons has his own proper relational function, we shall be saved from the excessive 'accommodationism' which is, for example, manifested

---

[1] Cf the long article by K. Rahner 'Theos in the New Testament' in *Theological Investigations* I, 78ff.
[2] Hebrews i, 3.
[3] Col. i, 15, 16.
[4] Hebrews i, 2.
[5] I Cor. viii, 6.

in the Anglican Catechism, which not only describes the activities of the Persons in terms of strict job-demarcation but also narrows down step by step the spheres of those activities: 'God the Father, who hath *made* me and *all the world* ..., God the Son, who hath *redeemed* me and *all mankind* ..., God the Holy Ghost, who *sanctifieth* me and *all the elect people of God.*' It is difficult to see how one could get closer to tritheism than this unless one explicitly declared that there were three Gods, and it is an alarming fact that for over four hundred years this has been the image of the Godhead which the Church of England has officially set before her children.

V

'— and from the Son': New Thought on an Old Dispute

No discussion of the Trinity could claim to be complete without some mention of the famous controversy about the *Filioque*. The basic issue can be stated quite briefly. In Dr Kelly's words:

> For many hundreds of years the text of C [the 'Niceno-Constantinopolitan' Creed] accepted in the Latin church and its daughter communions has contained the clause 'proceeding from the Father and the Son' (*filioque*) of the Holy Spirit. The Orthodox churches of the East have remained fiercely, even fanatically, attached to the more primitive 'proceeding from the Father'. A full discussion of the portentous addition in all its implications would necessitate an examination of at least three questions – the theology of the double procession, the history of the insertion of the *filioque*, and the history of the long-standing quarrel between East and West over it.[1]

The original reason for the introduction of the *filioque* seems very much of a mystery. It appears to have originated in Spain, but the view, once widely held, that it was adopted as a formula against the Arian heretics, who denied the deity of Christ, has recently been questioned. It is of course easy to argue that the violent antagonism which developed between East and West on the question was really an outcome of political and social ambitions and that there was

[1] J. N. D. Kelly, *Early Christian Creeds* (Longmans 1950), 358.

more eagerness to crystallize the theological issues into simple and inflexible slogans than to achieve mutual understanding and enrichment. Thus it has become common to set over against each other the formula of the Council of Florence that the Spirit proceeds from the Father and the Son 'as from one principle and by one spiration'[1] and Photius's formula that he proceeds 'from the Father alone', not as different insights to be diligently explored and assimilated but rather as contradictory ultimata to be accepted or rejected.

In recent years Anglicans have shown a readiness to consider eliminating the *filioque* from the Creed, but this must not be misunderstood. In so far as it is due to a recognition that the insertion of the term was uncanonical it may be applauded; and we may recall that Rome itself allows its omission in some of the uniate churches. And in so far as it is due to a considered doubt of the truth of the double procession it is certainly worthy of respect. I fear, however, that in most cases it is due to a complete lack of concern about the matter, frequently combined with great vagueness as to what exactly the doctrine is. All this stuff about the procession of the Spirit (these Anglicans say in effect) is incomprehensible and unimportant anyhow, but if dropping the *filioque* will mollify these quarrelsome Orthodox, then for goodness' sake let's do it. This attitude seems to me to be both short-sighted and offensive. As the distinguished Calvinist theologian Dr Alasdair Heron pointedly remarks, 'a willingness to jettison the *filioque* which rested on

[1] DS 1300.

nothing more than a sublime indifference to the whole matter would scarcely constitute a genuine step towards rapprochement with the East!'[1] I certainly do not despair of reconciling our differences, but the possibility depends on our first taking them seriously. If we make a genuine attempt to understand the different approaches of East and West to the Holy Spirit we may not only make some advance towards mutual reconciliation but may also deepen our own understanding of the Faith. But the first step must be to recover our own sense of the importance of orthodoxy with a small 'o', and we can hardly expect the Orthodox with a large 'O' to take us seriously about the procession of the Holy Spirit when we tolerate without protest the presence in high academic positions of Anglican priests who explicitly declare their disbelief in the Holy Trinity.[2] It is significant and deplorable, though not in fact surprising, that not one of the papers delivered at the high-level ecumenical consultations organized by the Faith and Order Commission of the World Council of Churches in October 1978 and May 1979 on the topic of the *Filioque* was by a professional Anglican theologian.

One of the most striking and encouraging facts that emerge from the published report of those consultations[3] is that Orthodox thought on the pro-

---

[1] *Spirit of God, Spirit of Christ*, ed. Lukas Vischer (London SPCK, Geneva WCC 1981), 112.

[2] Cf my *Whatever happened ...?*, ch. iv: 'Quicunque vult? Anglican Unitarians'.

[3] *Spirit of God, Spirit of Christ*, ed. Lukas Vischer (London SPCK, Geneva WCC 1981).

cession of the Spirit has not been limited to the simple profession of Photian monopatrism, the mere assertion that the Spirit proceeds 'from the Father alone', as if the begetting (generation) of the Son and the promission of the Spirit were two mutually insulated activities of the Father having, so to speak, no cross-reference to each other. The Greek Orthodox theologian Dr Markos Orphanos showed how Photius's thought was supplemented by Gregory of Cyprus, Gregory Palamas and Mark of Ephesus and how these thinkers made a vital distinction between the Procession (*ekporeusis*) of the Spirit, of which the Father is the sole cause (*aitia*), and his Manifestation (*ekphansis, phanerōsis, proeisis*), which is through the Son. This Manifestation, it is stressed, is within the eternal being of the Trinity and preceded God's manifestation of himself in creation, of which it provides the ground and possibility; and, in Palamas especially, the distinction between the Procession and the Manifestation is closely linked with the distinction between the divine Essence and Energies which is characteristic of the later Byzantine theology[1] but is very difficult to accommodate to our modes of thinking in the West.[2] It is, incidentally, surprising to discover that 'Palamas uses for the first time in the Greek patristic tradition the analogy of "love" (*erōs*) which was introduced in the West by Augustine and used by others.'[3] We are however warned that 'this

[1] Cf Lossky, *Mystical Theology*, ch. iv; J. Meyendorff, A Study of Gregory Palamas (Faith Press 1964), 202ff.

[2] Cf the discussion in my *Existence and Analogy* (Longmans 1949), 148ff.

[3] Orphanos in *Spirit of God* ..., 33.

characterization of the Holy Spirit as "love", used by the Father and the Son, applies not to the hypostasis of the Holy Spirit but to the common energy which is the love of the Triune God.'[1] Clearly, Dr Orphanos is not altogether easy with Palamas's 'appropriation' of love to the Spirit; he describes it as 'strange to the eastern tradition.'[2] And, in spite of Palamas's great authority among the Orthodox, this particular contribution does not seem to have met with much favour. Nor do the attempts of such modern Russian theologians as B. Bolotov and Sergius Bulgakov to make use, in this context, of the distinction between *dogmas*, which are essential and compulsory truths of the Faith, and *theologoumena*, which are very weighty but not absolutely mandatory views of theologians.[3] But there would certainly seem to be force in Bolotov's contention that the procession of the Spirit is causally, though of course not temporally, subsequent to the begetting of the Son:

> Although the Spirit does originate in the Father alone as the source of the divinity, he does not originate in the Father in isolation but in the one only Father as the unique Father of the only-begotten Son. The unique monarchy of the Father is manifested first of all in his unique generation of the only-begotten Son and, paradoxically, it is this latter generation which by its uniqueness guarantees that he is the unique principle of the Spirit in a radically different mode in the *ekporeusis*.[4]

[1] ibid., 34.
[2] ibid.
[3] B. Bobrinskoy in *Spirit of God* ..., 135f.
[4] *Spirit of God* ..., 153.

Thus the Roman Catholic writer Dom Jean-Miguel Garrigues, summarizing Bolotov in a very sympathetic survey. We might put by this the following passage from the widely read Calvinist theologian Dr Jürgen Moltmann; it is based on his study of Bolotov:

> If then God the Father breathes forth the Holy Spirit, the Spirit proceeds *from the Father of the Son*. His procession therefore presupposes (1) the generation of the Son, (2) the existence of the Son, and (3) the mutual relation of the Father and the Son. The Son is the logical presupposition and the material precondition for the procession of the Spirit from the Father, but he is not an additional accompanying source for him. The procession of the Spirit must be substantially distinguished from the generation of the Son by the Father.

Moltmann continues:

> If, furthermore, the Holy Spirit does not only proceed from the Father because the Father is the 'source of divinity', but because he is the Father of the only-begotten Son, then he derived also from the Fatherhood of God, that is, from the relation of the Father to the Son. While it is quite wrong to draw from this the further conclusion that the Spirit proceeds 'from the Father and the Son', one must hold equally firmly to the fact that the Spirit proceeds from the Father in the eternal presence of the Son, and that therefore the Son is not without a part in the matter.[1]

Thus, Moltmann proposes, we should speak of 'the Holy Spirit, who proceeds from the Father of the Son'; he wishes, however, to go further than this negative and remote reference to the Son and 'to advance from

---

[1] ibid., 168.

indirect circumscription to direct affirmation'. He picks up a well-known statement of Epiphanius in the fourth century, that the Spirit 'proceeds' from the Father and 'receives' from the Son, and he understands this 'receiving' as applying to the intra-trinitarian status of the Spirit and not just to his 'mission' in time. Specifically, Moltmann suggests that 'the Holy Spirit receives from the Father his own perfect divine *existence* (*hypostasis, hyparxis*), and obtains from the Son his relational *form* (*Gestalt*) (*eidos, prosōpon*) ...', and he asserts that 'when the theology of the eastern Church declares that the Holy Spirit proceeds from the Father 'alone' because the Father is 'the source of divinity', it only expresses the divinity of the *hypostasis* of the Holy Spirit over against every kind of divine creation, but not his inner-trinitarian and impersonal form.'[1]

Moltmann himself comments that 'the distinction here introduced between *hypostasis* and *prosopon*, or in Latin between *persona* and *facies*, may at first sight seem surprising', and I doubt whether this surprise will be altogether allayed by his explanation that 'if *hypostasis* is an ontological concept, *form* is an esthetic one', so that 'they do not compete with or replace each other, but are mutually complementary.'[2] However, Moltmann recommends as his revised interpretation the formula: 'The Holy Spirit, who proceeds from the Father of the Son and receives his form from the Father and from the Son.'[3]

[1] ibid., 169.
[2] ibid., 170.
[3] ibid., 171.

While I admire the dialectical skill with which Dr Moltmann pursues his pacific intentions, I feel doubtful of the wisdom of making a sharp contrast between two terms which since the fourth century have been taken as synonyms. To attempt a definitive assessment would need a discussion of his general philosophical position and at least some indication of the extent to which he views it as integral to his theology and of the extent to which he merely uses it as a convenient means of communication. I think this doubt underlies the comments made by the influential Rumanian theologian Dr Dumitru Staniloae in the concluding essay of the Consultation, in which he takes the statements of Fr Garrigues and Dr Moltmann as a starting-point. He is quite uncompromising in his rejection of the *filioque*, though he seems to be almost more concerned with the term than with its connotation. 'What you believe about the Holy Spirit may be quite sound', he appears to be saying, 'but I will not allow you to call it the *Filioque*.' 'Their viewpoints', he writes, 'seem to me to be a positive step towards the eastern doctrine even if, in some ways, an insufficient one. I shall therefore try to set out the eastern point of view in a positive way in order to bring a new contribution to the union of eastern and western Christianity on this subject.'[1] I shall however take as an exposition of his position not his contribution to the Consultation but the chapter on Trinitarian Relations and the Life of the Church in his

[1] ibid., 174.

book *Theology and the Church*,[1] in which he places trinitarian doctrine in the widest possible context. As we might expect, he starts from Gregory of Cyprus and Gregory Palamas but, in contrast to Dr Orphanos, he completes his triad of authorities not by Mark of Ephesus but by the fifteenth-century Byzantine writer Joseph Bryennios. As we might also expect from one who is much revered not just as an academic theologian but also as a teacher of the spiritual life, Staniloae bases his pneumatology not on a narrow and isolationist monopatrism but on our union with Christ through the Spirit in the Church. He gratefully welcomes the distinction made by the Gregories between the *Procession* of the Spirit and his *Manifestation*, and he also makes much of the Scriptural and patristic teaching that the Spirit 'comes to rest' on the Son. This 'abiding', which is an eternal and not just a temporal fact, both preserves the absolute prime causality of the Father and limits the number of the divine Persons. But – and here Palamas completes the teaching of the Cypriote – the Son is not just a passive recipient of the Father's love:

> The irradiation of the Spirit from the Son is nothing other than the response of the Son's love to the loving initiative of the Father who causes the Spirit to proceed. The love of the Father coming to rest in the Son shines forth upon the Father from the Son as the Son's love. It does not have its source in the Son but in the Father. When it falls upon the Son, however, it is shown to the Father; it is reflected back towards the Father, and joins

[1] Crestwood, N.Y., St Vladimir's Seminary Press 1980.

with the loving subjectivity which the Son has for the Father, in the same way that the Spirit of the Father who is communicated to us returns to the Father in conjunction with our own loving affection for him. This is so because the Son is not a passive object of the Father's love, as in fact we ourselves are not passive objects when the Holy Spirit is poured out upon us. The fact that it is through the Spirit that the Son loves the Father does not mean however that it is not he himself who loves the Father, and similarly, the fact that is is through the Spirit that we love the Father does not imply that it is not we ourselves who love him.[1]

We see here Staniloae's burning interest in theology as concerned with the welfare and fulfilment of actual men and women and not simply as a forum for the dialectical gymnastics of professional intellectuals. Thus he declares:

The Son of God became man not only to confer on us a general kind of divinity, but to make us sons of God. This is why the Son and no other Person of the Trinity became man, for, having the Spirit of the Son, he imparts this Spirit to us also so that we might have the Spirit in the Son and with the Son and thus be truly the sons of God and conscious of that fact.[2]

But now for Joseph Bryennios. His contribution, Staniloae tells us, was to recognize that, although the Son and the Spirit derive their existence from the two distinct causal acts of generation and promission respectively, this very fact involves a relation between them.

[1] *Theology and the Church*, 31.
[2] ibid., 33.

> Although this relation is not a causal one [i.e. the Son does not *cause* the Spirit], it is not on the other hand a purely essential relation [i.e. one arising simply from the fact that each of them shares the nature or essence of deity], but, according to Bryennios, derives from the fact that that the two Persons are differently caused by the Father and so indicates at one and the same time their common and different character as beings who have their causation from the same source and hence also their distinct personal character.[1]

Bryennios's teaching, as presented by Staniloae, becomes extremely complex. The upshot is, however, plain: 'Every relation between two Persons [of the Trinity] implies also the third Person', and 'the union between the Son and the Spirit consists first of all in the fact that the Spirit "shines forth" from the Son, and secondly that the Son as Word echoes back from the Spirit.' And this is the ground of the existence of the Christian and of the existence of the Church.

When the diligent Western student has reached this point he may well find himself wondering whether anything is left of the *filioque* controversy. Even the much abused Augustine and Aquinas, to whom, in alliance with the *Filioque*, the East has been accustomed to attribute most of the subsequent woes of the Church, were emphatic on the priority of the Father in the Trinity. And in view of the eagerness of the later Easterns to supplement the Photian monopatrism by affirming both the *promission* of the Spirit by the Father and his *manifestation* by the Son, may it not be possible to hold that both this promission and this manifestation

[1] ibid., 34.

are included in the one *procession* of the Spirit which the West ascribes without differentiation to 'the Father and the Son'? Does it really make sense to dispute whether these are two acts or two elements in one act? Admittedly, an obstacle might seem to arise, ironically enough, from the phrase which the Council of Florence hoped would conciliate the Easterns, when it affirmed that the Spirit proceeds from the Father and the Son 'as from one principle and by a unique spiration.'[1] Nevertheless, it could be argued that, although the *procession* (which can be understood as including both *promission* and *manifestation*) is from the two Persons, its *principle*, in the absolute, primary and unconditional sense of causal origin, is the Father alone; indeed, were this not so, the Spirit could not be described as proceeding 'as from one principle', since he would in fact be proceeding from two. Florence itself hints as much when, after asserting that the Son is what the Greeks call a 'cause' and the Latins a 'principle' of the subsistence of the Spirit, it goes on to say that this very fact of being one from whom the Spirit proceeds is conferred on the Son by the Father.[2]

Fr Jean-Miguel Garrigues has in fact maintained in

---

[1] The phrase (*tamquam ab uno principio et unica spiratione*), which is in the Bull of Union *Laetentur caeli* of 6 July 1439 (DS 1300), can be traced back at least to the Second Council of Lyons in 1274 (DS 850).

[2] *Filium quoque esse secundum Graecos quidem causam, secundum Latinos vero principium subsistentiae Spiritus Sancti, sicut et Patrem.... hoc ipsum quod Spiritus Sanctus procedit ex Filio, ipse Filius a Patre aeternitaliter habet* (DS 1301). Note that in Latin there is no definite or indefinite article.

an important recent study¹ that the common contrast between Greek East and Latin West is really an oversimplification; the 'Western' line has Alexandrian support, while the 'Eastern' is basically Cappadocian. The Cappadocian-Byzantine view sees in the generation of the Son the *negative condition* of the fact that the *ekporeusis* of the Spirit by the Father is not a second generation; the Latin-Alexandrian view sees in the generation of the Son the *positive condition* of the consubstantial procession of the Spirit in the communion of the Father and the Son. But both of these are really *theologoumena* upon the *dogma* that the Spirit is consubstantial with the Father.

Is it too much to hope, in view of all this, that we may be in sight of the moment when East and West will be able to agree that, stripped of their deplorable political aspects, the differences between them on the *Filoque* are largely verbal and conceptual and that, where they are substantial, they manifest varieties of insight which are not necessarily incompatible but, if they are offered and received with sympathy and understanding, may be mutually enriching and edifying? Can we hope for something comparable with the remarkable agreements on Christology that have been reached in the last few years between Rome and Orthodoxy on the one hand and the non-Chalcedonian or 'monophysite' Churches on the other.² Two con-

[1] *L'Esprit qui dit 'Père!': L'Esprit-Saint dans la vie trinitaire et le problème du filioque* (Paris, Téqui 1982); reviewed by Norman Russell in *Sobornost* VI-1 (1984).

[2] Cf my *Theology and the Gospel of Christ*, 146f, for references, and also (including later developments) Paulos Gregorios et al. edd., *Does Chalcedon Divide or Unite?* (Geneva, World Council of Churches 1981).

ditions are absolutely necessary. The first is that we in the West (and this means Anglicans in particular) shall cease to treat the *Filioque* as a trivial eccentricity, of interest only to theological antiquarians; it bears in fact on our intimate union with Christ. The second is that the Orthodox shall divest themselves of their tendency to ascribe to the *Filioque* almost everything that they have come to dislike in the West, natural theology, papal absolutism, the confusion of the Spirit with human subjectivity, and (almost entirely fictitious) the notion that grace is a purely created entity. Lossky, in a moving article published as long ago as 1948, suggested that the *filioque* was originally intended to express not the origination but the eternal manifestation of the Spirit and that even Augustine's filioquism might be taken in this sense; but, he regretfully continued, after the Councils of Lyons and Florence this was no longer possible. And then, he concluded, 'Western theologians had to profess the created character of glory and of sanctifying grace, to renounce the concept of deification; and in doing this they are quite consistent with the premises of their triadology.'[1] Both here and elsewhere[2] I have given reasons for questioning this last statement, and have shown that in the West Catholicism at any rate has held on both to deification and to uncreated grace against the attacks, often severe, of Protestantism. I

[1] Reprinted in *In the Image and Likeness of God* (Mowbrays 1975), 96.
[2] *He Who Is*, ch. x; *The Openness of Being* (Darton 1971), Appendix III: 'Grace and Nature in East and West'.

am fortified and enlightened by the wide-ranging and penetrating discussion given by Père Louis Bouyer in his brilliant work *Le Consolateur: Esprit Saint et Vie de grace*.[1] He comments sympathetically on the reservations which the Easterns feel about the specifically Augustinian features in Western trinitarian theology, their fear that in it not only the Spirit but all the three Persons are hardly personal at all; he instances Cajetan, who 'ends up by imagining a proper subsistence of the divine essence, anterior to those of the Three and independent of them.'[2] But this feature, he maintains, is widespread in the East also; he instances Evagrius, Basil, Gregory Nazianzen, Palamas and even Mark of Ephesus; of the Cappadocians, only Gregory of Nyssa is immune. And as teaching the priority of the Persons, Bouyer lists such undeniably Western figures as Gregory the Great, William of St-Thierry and, overshadowing them all, Thomas Aquinas.[3] On the *filioque* itself he makes the point that that the Latin *processio* embraces not only the Greek *ekporeusis* but also *proeisis*, not only origination but also manifestation;[4] but he carries through his real reconciliation of East and West in a detailed and profound study on the level of spirituality.[5]

To follow this out in detail would take us far from our immediate topic. But it is encouraging to notice that this last point of Bouyer's seems to be implicitly

[1] Paris, Cerf 1980.
[2] op. cit., 306.
[3] ibid., 307.
[4] ibid., 305; cf p. 60 above.
[5] ibid., 307ff.

endorsed in the first agreed statement, issued in August 1982, of the joint International Commission for Theological Dialogue between the Roman Catholic Church and the Orthodox Church which was established in December 1979. Its explicit subject was the Mystery of the Church and of the Eucharist in the light of the Mystery of the Holy Trinity. It asserts, without comment, that the Spirit 'proceeds eternally from the Father and manifests himself through the Son' and later affirms confidently that, 'without wishing to resolve yet the difficulties which have arisen between the East and the West concerning the relationship between the Son and the Spirit, we can already say together that the Spirit, which proceeds from the Father *as the sole source in the Trinity* and which has become the Spirit of our sonship *since he is also the Spirit of the Son*, is communicated to us particularly in the Eucharist by this Son, upon whom he reposes in time *and in eternity*.'[1] Again, Dr John Romanides, of the University of Thessalonica, addressing the Anglican-Orthodox Joint Doctrinal Commission in July 1982, drew a distinction between the 'cause of existence' of the divine Persons and the 'communication of essence' of the divine nature, and argued that, as concerned with the latter, the *Filioque* is an orthodox dogma and is found in Cyril of Alexandria, Maximus the Confessor and Anastasius the Librarian. Particularly significant is the assertion of the Report of this Commission that the experience

[1] *St Vladimir's Theological Quarterly*, XXVI-4 (1982), 252, 253, italics mine. The original document is in French.

of our participation in the grace of the Holy Trinity is the ultimate ground of any trinitarian doctrine and that 'if agreement could be reached on this, i.e. if it could be shown that Anglican and Orthodox Christians share the same experience of participation in God's saving grace, then the divergencies of doctrinal expression could be co-ordinated and appropriately resolved.'[1] Whatever areas of disagreement remain still to be explored, it is clear that recent years have seen a most striking drawing together on a matter which for centuries had been one of uncompromising confrontation, and with this the signs of renewal and enrichment in the life and thought of the Church. Most heartily I would applaud Lossky's fine aspiration:

> The Greeks have ceased to be Greeks in becoming sons of the Church. That is why they have been able to give to the Christian faith its imperishable theological armory. May the Latins in their turn cease to be solely Latins in their theology! Then together we shall confess our catholic faith in the Holy Trinity, who lives and reigns in the eternal light of his glory.[2]

---

[1] *Eastern Churches News Letter*, N.S. xvi (Spring 1983), 25f.
[2] *In the Image* ..., 96.

VI

Light from the Logicians

It is now high time for me to fulfil my promise[1] to apply to St Augustine's doctrine of the divine Persons as Substantial Relations some of the insights of modern logicians about relations as such. But first some clarification of St Augustine's doctrine itself may be useful, for the very notion of the Persons of the Trinity as 'relations' may seem ridiculous and indeed irreverent, whether qualified by an adjective or not. Do you really propose (it will be objected) to reduce the Lord Jesus and his heavenly Father and the Spirit who descended in tongues of fire at Pentecost to the status of logical concepts? Not at all, Augustine (and Aquinas) will reply; what I mean is that what constitutes each person as distinct from the others cannot be his substance, for each of them has the same identical substance, namely Deity; and it cannot be an accident or accidents, since accidents can be gained and lost, and the Persons, being divine, are imperishable and immutable. Therefore they can be constituted as distinct from one another only by their relations, but by relations which are as stable and firm as the divine substance itself. Perhaps 'relational subsistent' might have been a happier term than 'substantial relation'; Fr Jean Galot has suggested the terms 'relational being' (*être relationnel*) and 'hypostatic

[1] Cf p. 9 above.

relation'.[1] Constantly we must remind ourselves that we are speaking of transcendent realities which surpass our finite understanding, and that only by the divine mercy can we speak of them at all. It is only by our overhearing of the prayer of Jesus in the Gospels that we acquire some faint idea of the relation that unites and contrasts the Father and the Son.[2]

Next, it is normal, and in order to avoid confusion it is desirable, to distinguish between the *terms* which are linked by relations and the *relations* which link the terms, for example between the persons of the Father and the Son on the one hand and the relation of fatherhood and sonship on the other.[3] Yet we are told by Augustine that the Father *is* substantial Fatherhood and that the Son, correlatively, *is* substantial Sonship. Furthermore, since the Father promits the Spirit, it would seem to follow that he is substantial Promission as well as substantial Fatherhood; and now what has happened to his simplicity? We shall return to this, at least implicitly, later.

And here we must note an ambiguity for which the blame goes back to Aristotle but which has remained to our own time. Among the nine 'accidental' categories in the Aristotelian scheme, Relation, as we have seen, holds a unique place, in that, while each of the other eight simply attributes a characteristic to a

[1] (Gembloux, Duculot; Paris, Lethielleux, 1969), 41, 37.
[2] Cf my *Whatever happened to the Human Mind?* (SPCK 1980), 53f.
[3] It is a matter of definition whether fatherhood and sonship are considered as two relations or as one relation considered from two aspects. In formal logic, of course, they are two, and, assuming that the terms are male, each is the converse of the other.

subject, Relation involves a second term as well. To say that John is ugly speaks of nobody except John, but to say that John is uglier than Paul brings Paul into the picture as well. Nevertheless it *is* a statement about John and not a statement about Paul, though it does of course *imply* a statement about Paul, namely that Paul is less ugly than John. In other words, although it is of the essence of a relation that it associates *two* terms, it is in fact treated as a predicate of *one*.

Now it was a bright idea of A. N. Whitehead and Bertrand Russell at the beginning of this century, when they were engaged on their stupendous work *Principia Mathematica*, to interpret a relation between two terms as a predicate, but a predicate having two subjects instead of the usual one. Thus the statements about John and Paul just quoted would be seen as unphilosophical attempts to specify their functions as subjects of the dyadic predicate of comparative ugliness. (Later, Whitehead and Russell showed a tendency to reverse their procedure and rather to interpret a predicate as a special kind of relation, namely a relation having only one term instead of the usual two, but this is a comparatively minor point.) Furthermore, having the usual urge of mathematicians to generalize their concepts, they extended their theory to embrace relations between more than two terms, and predicates having more than two subjects.[1] (They had of course no intention or even suspicion that this might be useful in theology; what they were trying to do was

[1] B. Russell, *My Philosophical Development* (Allen & Unwin 1959), 99.

to reduce mathematics to a branch of logic. But it was Russell himself who made the famous remark that a mathematician never knows what he is talking about or whether what he is saying about it is true!) It is difficult to give this theory a precise description in words, for the simple reason that, in all languages commonly used by educated Europeans and Americans (I do not know about classical Chinese), a predicate has only one subject. But instances are plentiful. Thus Russell, after mentioning the relations of 'parent' and 'husband', continues:

> Such relations have two terms, and are called 'dyadic'. There are also relations of three terms, such as jealousy and 'between'; these are called 'triadic'. If I say 'A bought B from C for D pounds', I am using a 'tetradic' relation. If I say 'A minds B's love for C more than D's hatred of E', I am using a 'pentadic' relation. To this series of kinds of relation there is no theoretical limit.[1]

We notice, however, that this pentadic relation is expressed by a sentence which has the single *grammatical* subject A. Its meaning could be expressed in many other ways but each of these will have a single grammatical subject; one of them, for example, is 'C annoys A more by being loved by B than D does by hating E'. It is not surprising, therefore, that a philosopher, wishing to refer to a polyadic relation and to avoid as far as possible suggesting priority for one of its terms, will invent his own language and

[1] *Human Knowledge, its Scope and Limits* (Allen & Unwin 1949), 271.

denote it by a formula such as
$$R_n (x_1, x_2, x_3, \ldots x_n).[1]$$
But even the philosopher, when he wishes to expound and defend his theory, has to make use of written or spoken language, in which words are arranged in a one-dimensional sequence. It should be added that the existence of a polyadic relation does not exclude the existence of lower-order relations between some of its terms and may in fact entail them; in the pentadic case above, the dyadic relations of B's-love-for-C and D's-hatred-of-E also apply. But it is not, or is not necessarily, entailed by them: B might love C, and D might hate E, without A being concerned one way or the other.

Now, in applying these considerations to the theology of the Holy Trinity, I must make it plain that, although I am making use of human language and concepts, I am making use of them to talk about God and not about our ways of talking or of thinking about God. It is important to be clear about this because Aristotle's doctrine of the Categories was a doctrine about logic and language, whereas when Augustine and Aquinas used it in triadology it had become a doctrine about reality. Then, I am deeply conscious of the audacity which is involved in any attempt to penetrate the unfathomable mystery of the transcendent being of the triune God. My excuse is that provided by the opening words of the Epistle to the Hebrews, that God, who of old time spoke to the

[1] Cf B. Russell, *An Enquiry into Meaning and Truth* (Allen & Unwin 1940), 95.

Fathers by divers portions and in divers manners by the prophets, has in these last days spoken to us in a Son; and it is by that utterance that I would wish my own feeble stammerings to be judged. If they fail the test, the sooner they are forgotten the better.

Having said this, I will make the suggestion that we should consider the three divine Persons as the three subjects of a concrete triadic relation by which God exists as supreme reality in trinitarian being. In that triadic relation each of the subjects has his own uninterchangeable place, function and contribution, yet each exists and functions only in view of his relation as co-subject with the other two. I must be precise on this point. I do not mean that the Persons have various dyadic relations in pairs to one another and that their trinitarian relation is obtained by adding these together or abstracting some common element from them. That there are such dyadic relations of course I admit; they are of enormous importance: the Father eternally begetting the Son, the Spirit promitted by the Father, and so on. But antecedent to them all is the primordial triadic relation by which all three are the triune God. It is, I believe, the intuition of this fact that led the *Quicunque vult*, after it had systematically specified the dyadic relations of the Persons each to each, to draw them together by declaring that 'in this Trinity there is nothing before or after, nothing greater or less, but all three Persons are coeternal with each other and coequal.' (The misfortune was that the only polyadic relation envisaged was equality.) The *Quicunque* draws the safe and orthodox conclusion that 'both trinity in unity and unity in trinity must be worshipped.' Too often, however, an emphasis upon the dyadic relations of the Persons has led to some form or other of subordinationism, and then, in reaction, a stress on the equality of the Persons has produced the image of the Trinity as a council of three with equal voting powers. Both these extremes are, in their opposite ways, unbalanced and over-simplified; an understanding of the triadic relation of the divine Persons might have preserved the truth and excluded the error in both. I will give as a specific example the controversy about the *filioque*.

I will leave it to those who are more learned in patristic studies than I am to argue whether and when there were some Greek fathers who accepted the *filioque* and some Latin fathers who denied it, and whether the Greeks meant by *aitia* and *ekporeusis* precisely what the Latins meant by *causa* and *processio*; not that I think those issues are unimportant and I have devoted a good deal of space to them in the last chapter. I do not think that all the arguments adduced were frivolous or trivial, though they cannot all have been correct. It is natural that in the earlier stages phrases were used that were incorrect by later standards, and avenues explored which turned out to be blind alleys. But I suggest that some tensions might have been eased if it had been remembered that the three divine Persons live in a triadic relation and not just in a set of dyadic ones. 'The Father is the source of Godhead', say the Greeks, 'and he eternally begets the son.' 'Of course;' say the Latins, 'we agree.' 'And then,' the Greeks continue, 'he eternally promits the Spirit.' 'Well, yes,' the Latins somewhat hesitantly reply, 'but doesn't the Son come into that too? Didn't many of your Greek fathers say that the Spirit proceeds from the Father through the Son?' 'Yes,' the Greeks rejoin, 'but you say he proceeds from the Father *and* the Son; you make the Son a second source of Godhead.' 'No, no,' the Latins protest, 'we made that clear at Florence when we said "as one principle and by a unique spiration".' 'What?!' comes the outraged cry of the Greeks, '*two* divine Persons *one* principle? You must be joking to confuse them like that. We stand by the blessed Photius – "from the Father *alone*"!' 'Then,' whisper the Latins in honeyed tones, 'what about Gregory of Cyprus and the eternal manifestation of the Spirit by the Son?' And so the argument continues, with little prospect of ending. May the heart of the problem lie in a failure to recognize that, behind the dyadic relations of begetting, promission, origination, manifestation and the rest, there lies the primal trinitarian relation, not dyadic but triadic, whose three subjects are the Father, the Son and the Holy Spirit, none of whom can be adequately spoken of except in the context of the other two. (In symbols this might be expressed by the formula

$$D (P, F, S)$$

where 'D' stands for *Deus* and 'P', 'F' and 'S' for *Pater*, *Filius* and *Spiritus* respectively, though with the proviso that this only indicates the triadicity of the relation and tells us nothing about its character.) The doctrine of *perichoresis* or *circumincession*, of the mutal interpenetration and indwelling of the three Persons, in which the debate about the Trinity culminated in the early Church, is rightly judged as the keystone which holds the fabric of triadology together. But it is only from the historical aspect that it should be seen as the result of a tidying-up operation and as a final cosmetic ornamentation of the doctrinal structure. Ontologically its place is at the beginning, not at the end; this is one of the many cases where the order of being is the inverse of the order of discovery. It is a statement in theological metaphysics and not in the psychology of theologians; that is to say, it is an assertion, admittedly obscure and analogical as all such assertions must be, about God, and not about how some people have thought about God. But, furthermore – and it is here that what has been said about polyadic relations is relevant – I would maintain that it has not only metaphysical but also *noetic* significance; that is that it provides not only a *de facto* description but expresses the very *meaning*, of the triadic relation in which the three Persons stand.

There is thus altogether excluded that view of God as an impersonal divine essence, antecedent to its differentiation into the Persons, of which, justly or unjustly, Easterns have frequently accused the West. There is no God other than the Father, the Son, and the Holy Spirit, as subjects of the triadic trinitarian relation. But equally there is excluded any notion of the Persons, or any of them, enjoying an individual status independent of, or antecedent to, his union with the other two in that relation. I accept, of course, the dyadic relations which are classical in Christian theism, for example that by which the Father eternally begets the Son. If, however, we remember that, in virtue of their common deity and equality, the filiality of the Son is as basic as the paternity of the Father,[1] and if we remember, as East and West agree, that the Holy Spirit is the mutal love and the bond of love between the Father and the Son,[2] we may be able to see these dyadic relations as included within the basic and comprehensive triadic trinitarian relation whose co-subjects are the Father, the Son and the Holy Spirit. Even so, we must recognize that the one-dimensional character of human discourse imposes on all our statements about the Trinity the grammatical and syntactical handicap of having one (grammatical) subject and not three.[3] Thus the statement just made about the bond of love between the Persons had the syntactical form of statement *about* the Spirit; it could be replaced without change of meaning by a statement about either of the other Persons (e.g. 'The Father is bound in mutual love with the Son by the Holy Spirit') but not by a statement which is syntactically about

---

[1] This is the point made by Dr Torrance; cf p. 41 above.

[2] Dr Boris Bobrinskoy writes: 'This idea, which is perhaps inspired by the psychological analogies of St Augustine, turns up again in the East in St Gregory Palamas in the fourteenth century, but replaced in an Orthodox *Trinitarian context*' (*Spirit of God* ..., 142).

[3] This is true even when the grammatical subject is a noun in the plural number.

all three. If we forget these inherent limitations of language as such we may find ourselves importing into our trinitarian theology false priorities and imbalances which only a subsequent more discriminating examination may discern. It may be an intuition of this fact that leads Dr Bobrinskoy, in one of the most penetrating and sympathetic discussions of the *filioque* dispute that I have seen in any Orthodox writer, to write *à propos* of this very point:

> I would add that in Orthodox consciousness of the Trinity, it is not only the Holy Spirit who has the 'prerogative' to be the link between the divine hypostases. Each hypostasis gathers together and unites the others in himself, the Father as source in the monarchy, the Son as the One in whom the Father and the Spirit find their resting place.[1]

But to this I would myself wish to add that the primordial truth about the divine unity is not that there are three 'links' by which each of the Persons holds together in himself the other two, but that there is one tripersonal embrace in which these dual links are subsumed. Whether others will find the analogy of triadic relations as helpful as I have found it I do not know, but it seems to me to preserve and to unify the two essentials of a sound trinitarian theory, namely the primary and concrete reality of the three divine Persons and the unity, both numerical and ontological, of God. More than that I would not wish to claim.

As I come to the end of this discussion, I am more than usually conscious of the danger of presumption

[1] *Spirit of God* ..., 142.

that threatens any human attempt to depict the face of God. But I return to the assurance that, although no man has seen God at any time, the only-begotten Son, who is in the bosom of the Father, has declared him. And I know that to share the life of the triune God is the end for which I am made and that I have already begun to enjoy it, since grace is nothing else than the beginning of glory is us.[1] So I will end by quoting two passages. The first is from the final canto of the *Paradiso*, in which Dante affirms the totally satisfying character of the vision of the triune Deity, of which he claims to have been granted an all but inexpressible glimpse:

And so my mind, bedazzled and amazed,
  Stood fixed in wonder, motionless, intent,
  And still my wonder kindled as I gazed.

That light doth so transform a man's whole bent
  That never to another sight or thought
  Would he surrender, with his own consent;

For everything the will has ever sought
  Is gathered there, and there is every quest
  Made perfect, which apart from it falls short....

High phantasy lost power and here broke off;
  Yet, as a wheel moves smoothly, free from jars,
  My love and my desire were turned by love,

The love that moves the sun and the other stars.[2]

[1] *S. Theol.* II II, xxiv, 3 ad 2. Cf my *Grace and Glory* (SPCK 1975), ch. i.

[2] *The Comedy of Dante Alighieri*, trans. Dorothy L. Sayers and Barbara Reynolds (Penguin 1962), III, 346f.

The other passage is from Jacques Maritain's introduction to Fr Bruno's study *St John of the Cross*:

> Brother Albert of the Virgin, porter of the Convent of the Martyrs, was on the point of death. His countenance was aflame, and shone with a celestial light which rendered it so marvellously beautiful that all were enraptured and silently shed tears of joy.... Suddenly Brother Albert cried out in a loud voice: 'Ah! I have seen it, Ah! I have seen it, Ah! I have seen it,' and immediately lowering his arms, crossed them on his breast. As he was about to close his eyes, our Venerable Father John of the Cross hastened to ask him this question: 'Brother Albert, what have you just seen?' and he answered 'Love, love,' and remained in an ecstasy.[1]

---

[1] op. cit., xvi.

www.ingramcontent.com/pod-product-compliance
Lightning Source LLC
Chambersburg PA
CBHW072011090426
42734CB00033B/2457